Concepts for
Effective Offense

Steve Axman

ISBN: 1-58518-953-7
Library of Congress Control Number: 200593831

Book layout: Bean Creek Studio
Diagrams: Chasity Seibert
Cover design: Jeanne Hamilton
Front cover photo: Harry How/Getty Images

Coaches Choice
P.O. Box 1828
Monterey, CA 93942
www.coacheschoice.com

Dedication

To Marie, my wonderful wife and best buddy!

Acknowledgements

Much of the material in this book was taught to be by my truest mentor, Homer Smith. Although I coached for Homer over a quarter century ago, the concepts he taught me about offensive football hold as true today as they did over 25 years ago.

I must also acknowledge such tremendous personal teachers as Lindy Infante, Darryl "Mouse" Davis, Larry Smith, Joe Krevak, Jack Elway, Jim McNally, Ted Williams, and Keith Gilbertson. I would also like to acknowledge some fine assistants who worked with me when I was the head coach at Northern Arizona University and who helped to develop some of the conceptual thinking in this book: Karl Darrell, Steve Kragthorpe, and Ken Zampese. Special acknowledgement from that fine group of coaches goes to Brent Myers. All of these coaches have had a profound impact on my offensive thinking.

Introduction

101 Concepts for Effective Offense will present the reader with 101 theoretical, and yet practical, concepts for effective offensive football. Each mini-concept deals with a particular aspect of offense. While many of the concepts do flow in a consistent, related fashion in which one concept builds upon another, the concepts are listed numerically in an effort to present an orderly presentation. However, a concept may be concerned with a totally different subject than the one preceding it. Concepts will be grouped together thematically. As a result, run play concepts will be grouped together as will pass route and pattern concepts. Early in the book, the concepts all tie into the central theme of multiplicity. Such a grouping of concepts is done in an effort to tie together the total knowledge presentation of each concept whenever possible.

The offensive concepts are theoretical in nature. Coaches may differ, wholly or partially, with the thinking of some of the concepts. Hopefully, the reader will be able to find some form of helpful information. Some of the concepts may be of little to no use to a coach because of the style (or type) of offense that he uses. If a coach does not use the option run game, then such concepts may be of little or no use to him. However, in reading over the information concerning such concepts, a coach might have a light turned on. He just may find a fresh, new concept to add to his offensive thinking to help him attack opposing defenses. Other concepts surely could have been added to, or included in, this presentation. In all, it certainly was the intent of the author to present a clear and complete conceptual presentation in regard to *101 Concepts for Effective Offense*.

Contents

Concept #1: Play offensive football that is truly offensive!

Think of a person who has an offensive personality. Think of someone who is a little nasty, a little surly, a little arrogant. He is the type of person who, as a player, would enjoy knocking a person down and running over the top of him as much as he would scoring or winning a game. That's the type of personality you need to have as an offensive coach. That is the type of personality your offense, your players, need to have. You need to make sure that your offense plays the game with an attitude that truly is offensive. It is a personality, an attitude that works hard to find the weaknesses of a defense and then pounds away to exploit those weaknesses in an effort to get the opposition to surrender.

Knute Rockne-type words, you say? Perhaps. However, it's amazing to see how many offensive coaches approach offense with an attitude that's defensive in nature: "We can't run this! We can't run that! They'll shut that down!" Before you know it, they hardly have anything left on their call sheet to run. Maybe they will shut parts of your offense down. That's not the question. The question is, "What can your offense do to be successful versus an opponent's defense?" Your attitude must be to find ways to be successful versus your opponents. Find their weaknesses and go for the jugular. They're going to find ways to shut down your bread-and-butter off-tackle power play? Then find a new formation, motion, or shift that will eliminate the ability of the defense to overload in an effort to stop your best play. When your offense is in possession of the football, it's not time to focus on what you can't do. It's time to figure out what you can (and must) do to be successful. It's time to attack. It's time to be offensive.

Concept #2: Force the defense to play on its heels.

Defenses are rhythmic. They want to read and react. Defenses don't want, or like, to think. They like to play up on the balls of their feet, ready to fly and pursue to the football. Defenses don't like to sit back on their heels making checks to motions, shifts, and formation alignment variations.

A major key for an offense is to not let a defense zero in on it. An offense wants to make the defense think. It wants to make the defense frown. "Check the shift. Check the shift. You have the slot. Motion, motion! I have him! I have him!" That's the type of verbiage you want to hear a linebacker call out in response to a multiplicity of offensive movement and formation change. Force the defense to play back on its heels, not up on the balls of its feet.

Concept #3: Don't use pro right and left formation.

The statement "Don't use pro right and left formation" is a complete exaggeration. The pro set formation has been around football for a long time. It will probably continue to be around football for an even greater amount of time. Its problem is that it is the offensive formation off of which almost every defense bases its design. Open up any defensive playbook and it is almost guaranteed that all of the base fronts, coverages, stunts, and blitzes are drawn up against a pro set formation. Any other formation, or alignment variation, becomes a defensive adjustment. In most cases, it is preferable to play against a defense's adjustments than its base defense. When playing outside of its base design, a defense potentially has to make adjustments for every front, coverage, stunt, and blitz it uses. As a result, instead of an "up on the balls of the feet," read-and-react defense, the defense is forced to sit back "on its heels" and think of how it must adjust to non-pro set formations.

Some years ago, we went into spring practice with the goal of not using a single pro set formation. After two weeks, the head coach asked me if I would put the pro set formation back into our offensive package *for the defense*. The defense had complained that all they were playing was "adjustment" defense against us. They hadn't been in their base defense one time to that point in the spring practice.

Adjustment defense is what you want to play against. Take the defense out of the comfort zone of its base design. The defense isn't zeroing in on the offense when its major concern is getting properly aligned on an offensive formation other than a pro set. Quite the opposite is taking place. Again, the pro set formation does have excellent usages. You just want it to be your base offensive formation, thereby allowing the defense the comfort of being able to play its base defensive design. Diagram 3-1 shows a typical pro set formation that is the basis for the design of so many defenses.

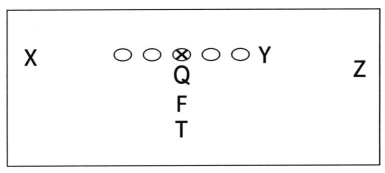

Diagram 3-1. Pro set formation

Concept #4: Apply your base run/pass offense with a multiplicity of formations, personnel plans, shifts, and motions.

An excellent means of attacking a defense is by being multiple. Using a large variety of offensive alignments creates lots of problems for a defense. Multiplicity of offense forces a defense to be in an adjustment mode. Motions, shifts, and a variety of formations and personnel plans help to create situations that can be very advantageous to the offense.

A key factor to the success of such offensive multiplicity is to be sure that the total offensive package utilized is not too large for the offense to be able to execute and handle. When utilizing a multiple offense approach, the mistake that many coaches make is to use a large variety of different plays. Play execution is paramount to total offensive execution. Utilizing 15 or 20 runs and 25 to 30 passes does not help to produce precise play execution. In addition, such a large play package often seems to produce a bunch of fragmented plays that, very often, do not complement one another in integrated run and pass play packages. It almost seems that the running or passing game design becomes a conglomeration of the best plays of other people's offenses rather than an integrated package of plays that complement and feed off of one another.

The key to effective multiple offense is to apply a tight, well-designed, simple base run and pass package with a wide variety of formations, personnel packages, shifts, and motions. In this fashion, the same base runs and passes are executed over and over but from consistently different looks. Once again, this approach forces the defense to play adjustment defense, even though the offense is simply applying its base offense in a wide variety of ways. The defense may very well be trying to stop your top run play, the toss sweep. However, by utilizing your toss sweep from a variety of formations, personnel plans, shifts, and motions, the run play can be well disguised so that the defense is not fully ready to take the play on when it is run. Multiplicity can also help the offense to make its own needed adjustments to best attack the defense it is facing, as well as to make the best use of its talent by allowing the football to be in the hands of its most talented players.

Concept #5: Use multiple formations.

Multiple formations are an easy, and greatly beneficial, way to produce effective multiple offense. Even with a simple variety of formations, the defense is forced to react and adjust to the offense. Some coaches believe in mixing their formation structure on (almost) every down in an effort to keep the defense off balance. The offense can take the process one step further and add the factor of varied personnel plans within the multiple formation application. When varied personnel plans are used along with varied formations, the multiple offense concept effect becomes magnified to an even greater degree. Such action helps to keep the defense "thinking" rather than being able to sit comfortably and simply read and react.

   Diagram 5-1 shows how a pro right formation can provide tremendous variation by simply aligning (shifting) the tailback in a variety of positions. Actually, the fullback could be easily used to accomplish the same formation alignment variations as well. Or, a personnel plan change can be made, substituting a third wide receiver slotback for either the tailback or fullback.

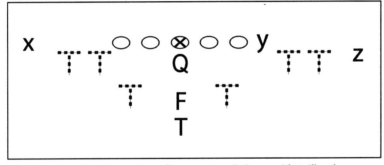

Diagram 5-1. Pro formation alignment variations with tailback

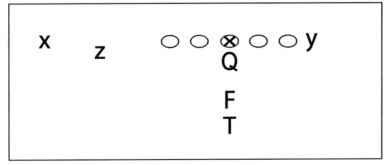

Diagram 5-2. Pro personnel plan twins formation

   Diagram 5-2 shows a pro right formation flanker aligning in the slot to the split end side to produce an entirely different, and yet simple, pro personnel plan twins formation variation. This change may not seem like a major one for the offense.

However, it presents a very different formation problem for the defense due to the change of strength of the offense.

Diagram 5-3 shows how the simple flexing of a pro personnel plan tight end can give the defense the problems of a three-wide receiver spread formation. Diagram 5-4 shows a pro personnel plan tight end flexed out as a wide receiver (in a normal split end alignment) away from a twins alignment set. Such a formation creates a whole new set of problems for the defense through simple formational alignment variations

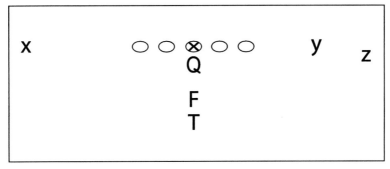

Diagram 5-3. Pro personnel plan with flexed tight end

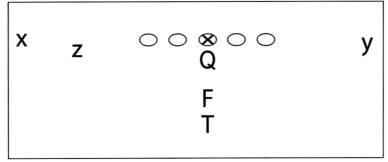

Diagram 5-4. Pro personnel plan twins formation with tight end flexed out to a wide receiver alignment.

Such formation multiplicity can go on and on. Trips, quads, no backs, and shotgun are but a few of the many varied multiple formation concepts that an offense can utilize. It is important to note, however, that an offense should use a formation for a reason other than to just be multiple. What does a twins formation do for you? How does the opposition's defense react to the twins set? What advantage does using the twins formation give you? If it doesn't give you an advantage, then you probably shouldn't use it.

Concept #6: Use multiple personnel plans.

Just as multiple formations greatly help to easily produce effective multiple offense, so does the use of varied personnel plans. With varied personnel plan usage, the defense is forced to react and adjust to each new and different plan. (A plan is the grouping of personnel to be used for a particular reason. A pro personnel plan has two wide receivers, a tight end, and two backs. A trio plan could be the name given to the personnel plan that has three wide receivers, a tight end, and one back.)

Today's football is very "match-up" oriented. An extra wide receiver brings into the game an extra nickelback secondary defender. By mixing personnel structure liberally, the defense is once again kept off balance. The offense is forcing the defense to react to the action of the offense. Add to the mixture of personnel plans a good variety of formations and the multiple offense concept is magnified to an even greater degree. Just as in the defensing of each and every formation, the defense now has to add the additional concern of adjusting every front, coverage, stunt, and blitz it is using to not only the formation being utilized, but the particular personnel plan that is manning the offense at that time.

Diagram 6-1 shows a trips to the flanker formation. The slotback could be a pro personnel plan fullback or tailback. The slotback could also be the third receiver from a three-wide-receiver, one-tight-end, one-back personnel plan. Another possibility is for the slotback to be the second tight end in a two-wide-receiver, two-tight-end, one-back personnel plan. The defense may be getting the exact same formational look. However, it must still contend with the actual personnel being utilized by the offense at the time.

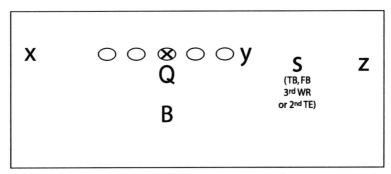

Diagram 6-1. Trips to the flanker formation with varied personnel plans

Diagram 6-2 shows a one-wide-receiver, two-tight-end (extra "U" tight end), two-back personnel plan with an I tight formation. Diagram 6-3 shows a three-wide-receiver, two-back personnel plan with a slot formation strong and a split end backside. Diagram 6-4 shows a four-wide receiver, one-back personnel plan with a double slot formation. Diagram 6-5 shows a five-wide receiver, empty formation. Each of the formations can be utilized by using varied personnel plans. Diagram 6-6 shows the same empty formation shown in Diagram 6-5 using pro plan personnel.

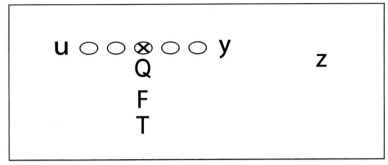

Diagram 6-2. I tight formation with a one-wide-receiver, two-tight-end, two-back personnel plan

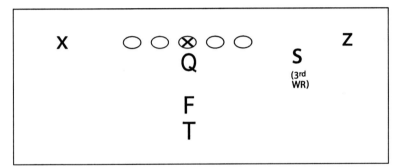

Diagram 6-3. Slot formation with a three-wide-receiver, two-back personnel plan

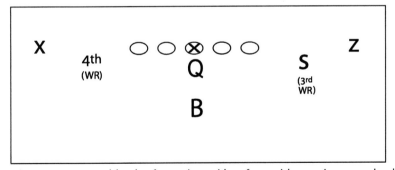

Diagram 6-4. Double slot formation with a four-wide-receiver, one-back personnel plan

Personnel plan multiplicity, tied into the concept of multiple formation usage, can produce an almost endless amount of multiple offense variety. However, just as in the usage of multiple formations, using a particular personnel plan should be done for a sound reason (other than just to be multiple). What does pro personnel do for you?

How about two-wide-receiver, two-tight-end, one-back personnel? How about five-wide-receiver, empty action? What advantage does a particular personnel plan give you? If a personnel plan does not give you an advantage, then why use it?

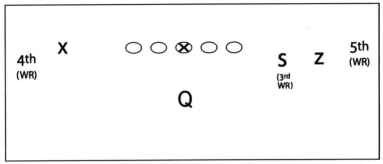

Diagram 6-5. Empty formation with a five-wide-receiver personnel plan

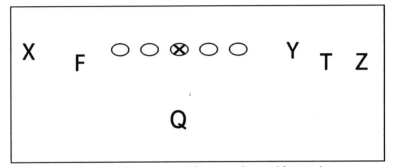

Diagram 6-6. Empty formation with a pro (two-wide-receiver, one-tight-end, two-back) personnel plan

Concept #7: Use shifts and motions to add to offensive multiplicity.

The next concept that can be very useful in helping to produce an effective multiple offense is the use of shifting and motioning. Such actions force the defense to react and adjust to actual changes in alignments and/or formations helping to keep the defenses off balance. Some shifts and motions will force the defense (or certain defenders) to soften—or loosen—their alignments due to fears of being susceptible to certain types of blocking angles created by such shifts and motions. Such shifts and motions may even change the strength of the formation, definitely a major concern for the defense. And, mixing shifting and motioning with formation and personnel variation helps to magnify the multiple offense concept effect to its greatest degree.

Diagram 7-1 shows the use of shifting to create a pro formation change of strength. Diagram 7-2 shows a short motion action by an I formation fullback to put him in a better position to toss sweep arc block a strong safety.

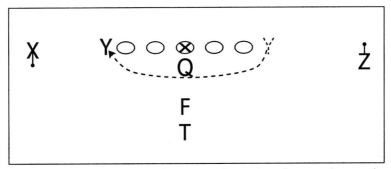

Diagram 7-1. Shifting to produce a pro formation change of strength

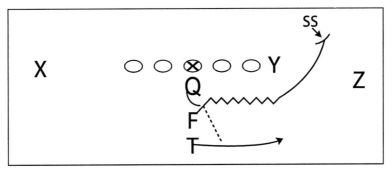

Diagram 7-2. Short motion by I fullback to produce better blocking angle on toss sweep

Much like multiple offense formation variation and variety of personnel plans, the use of shifting and motioning should be used for sound and definite reasons. The reasons may be only for disguise or distraction. However, if no advantage can be seen in such shift and motion usage, there really is little reason to use it.

Concept #8: Shifts and motions can help create mismatches.

One of the best uses of shifting and/or motioning is to help create personnel mismatches. This situation is often seen when an offense uses shifting and/or motioning to change formation strength. Many defensive front structures do not have the flexibility to swap personnel when such a change of formation strength is made. As a result, a smaller, faster open-side rush defensive end may suddenly find himself being covered by, and being forced to play on, a big, shifted tight end. Suddenly, the defensive end's speed may be negated and his size a disadvantage versus the blocking of a larger, more physical blocker. Diagram 8-1 shows the creation of a blocking mismatch on a smaller, openside rush defensive end through the shifting of a pro formation tight end from one side of the formation to the other.

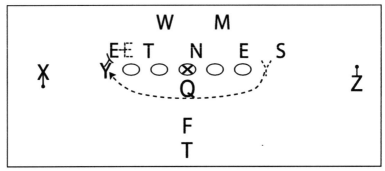

Diagram 8-1. Shifting to create a personnel mismatch

Concept #9: Motions can help to declare whether the coverage is zone or man.

Motioning can be an excellent tool to help determine whether a pass coverage is a zone coverage or a man-to-man coverage. This advice is especially true when the motion receiver crosses the formation to force the defense to declare what it is doing. If the defender covering the crossing-the-field motioning receiver runs across the formation with the receiver, the chances are extremely high that the defense is using man-to-man coverage. If the secondary bumps its secondary across the field with the crossing-the-field motioning receiver, the chances are extremely high that the defense is using a zone coverage. Coverages could disguise and dummy such actions. However, they would have to be extremely sophisticated to do so. Diagram 9-1 shows the use of cross-the-formation motioning in an attempt to determine whether the defense is using man-to-man or zone coverage.

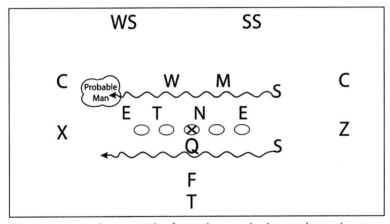

Diagram 9-1. Using cross-the-formation motioning to determine zone or man-to-man coverage

Concept #10: Use irregular formations from specific personnel plans to heighten multiplicity.

Another means of heightening, or magnifying, the multiple offense concept is to use what the defense would view as irregular formations from specific personnel plans. In essence, the defense ends up facing a formation they would not expect to see once they have determined from the offensive substituting what the offensive personnel plan is. Once again, the defense is put in a situation where they must react and adjust to what the offense is doing. Such irregular formation usage can definitely help to keep the defense off balance.

Often, when seeing such an irregular formation for the first time, a defense may very well misalign or pass cover the formation incorrectly. This reaction can help to produce mismatches in favor of the offense. It is very important for a multiple offense to have a definite reason for using such irregular formations. From a pass design, the pass patterns themselves should reflect a means of taking advantage of defensive miscues in regard to defensing an irregular formation. Quarterback hand signaling can help put receivers in route combinations that can most effectively attack the coverage seen. Utilizing "check-with-me" signals can help an irregular formation take advantage of any defensive alignment or coverage mistakes with both the running and the passing game.

Diagram 5-4 showed an irregular set from pro personnel. The tight end is shown splitting out in what would normally be a split end set away from a slotted twins set of the normal split end and flanker. Diagram 10-1 shows a no backs formation, also from pro personnel, in which the two pro personnel backs align out wide as wide receivers. The question becomes, "How does the defense play these widely split running backs? How does the defense play the normal wide receivers who are now aligned inside in slotted type alignments?" These types of multiple offense concepts can greatly, and easily, help to produce effective multiple offense.

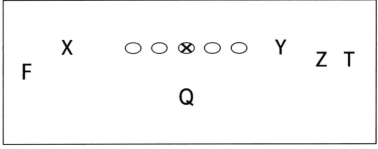

Diagram 10-1. Irregular empty formation from pro personnel plan

Concept #11: Multiplicity often helps cut down on defensive volume.

Multiple offense often has the effect of forcing a defense to cut down on its total volume. For every formation or personnel plan utilized, the defense must be sure that all its fronts, coverages, secondary run supports, stunts, and blitzes are able to efficiently and effectively defense each offensive variation. If an offense motions one of its wide receivers across the formation, how does the defense react? How does it adjust a particular front stunt that has been called in the defensive huddle? How does the defense adjust a blitz called, or the front called, or a specific coverage? The answer might be that the defense doesn't. Often, the defense will react by canceling a called stunt or blitz. Or, it may go to automatic adjustments and coverage changes. More often than not, a defensive staff will cut down on its volume in the game-planning stage during the week prior to the game when facing a multiple offense.

Most defensive coaches design their defensive package around the concept of simplicity. Keep It Simple, Stupid (KISS) is an often used defensive motto. Keep the defensive structure simple so that the defensive players can read, react, and fly to the football. Confusion on the football field—whether on offense, on defense, or in the kicking game—usually has disastrous results. As a result, when a defense faces an offense that is multiple, the thinking by the defense is to often cut back on defensive volume in that important effort to "keep it simple" and avoid confusion and mistakes.

Concept #12: Defenses do not like to see wing sets.

Defenses do not like to see wing set formations. Some defenses may feel compelled to defense such wing sets with secondary personnel who do not normally play line-of-scrimmage alignments and techniques. A wing set often produces an abnormal line-of-scrimmage power set that can quickly outflank a defense if not defensed correctly. In addition, many defenses almost act uncertain concerning how to align on a wing set due to the variety of run schemes and pass route combinations that a wing set can impose. Thus, aligning on a wing set can quickly allow for offensive advantages in regard to attacking defensive weaknesses.

Once again, the defense may be forced, due to defensive design, to defense the wing alignment with secondary support personnel. This action may be very uncommon for such defenders. Whether the wing set is defensed by secondary defenders or defenders from the defensive front, the wing set alignment variation can help to produce defensive confusion and uncertainty. Such action can help create a possible advantage for the offense to exploit. Diagram 12-1 shows a one-back formation wing set with slotted receivers to the opposite side.

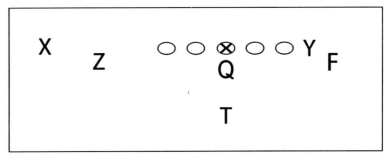

Diagram 12-1. One-back wing set formation

Concept #13: Defenses do not like to see two- and three-tight-end personnel plans and formations with two backs in the backfield.

Defenses do not like to see two- and three-tight-end personnel plans and formations that have two backs in the backfield. Much like wing sets, the extra tight end personnel helps create alignment and technique play adjustment problems for the defense. A major reason for this is that secondary defenders are often forced to play alignments and techniques that they are not normally accustomed to playing. This problem is compounded by the fact that smaller secondary defenders are often forced to play tightly on big tight end personnel offenders. In addition, the defense is forced to be concerned about normal two-back run offense while still concerning itself with the problems that two- and three-tight-end formations and alignments can present to the defense. (One-back offense can also be very effective when using two- and three-tight-end personnel. However, having two backs in the backfield does help the offense to give the defense a much larger variety of run threats with which to contend.)

In essence, the use of two or three tight ends with two backs in the backfield can distort the defensive structure, helping to produce physical mismatches in favor of the offense—especially in the run game. Of course, the defense can make personnel substitutions of its own to match up (especially physically) with the offense. However, unless it is for a key critical situation need, such as third-and-short or coming out offense, a defense may be unwilling to make such personnel substitution changes out in the field. Diagram 13-1 shows a three-tight-end, two-back personnel wing set formation.

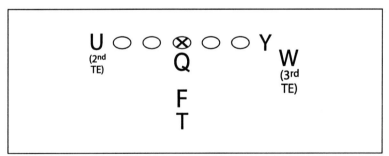

Diagram 13-1. Three-tight-end, two-back personnel formation with third tight end wing set

Concept #14: Defenses do not like to see unbalanced formations.

Defenses do not like to see unbalanced formations, especially when the offense leaves a tight end on the short backside. When this is done, the unbalanced formation leaves a legitimate pass receiving threat on the backside for the defense to have to contend with. Unbalanced formations distort defenses. If the defense shifts over one man in an effort to balance the defense up to the unbalanced formation, the front defenders end up aligning and playing their techniques on offenders that they normally do not work off of. In the secondary, the defense may have to contend with an extra receiver threat, especially if a tight end or wide receiver is not left on the backside of the unbalanced formation.

The use of unbalanced formations greatly helps to promote multiple offensive thinking. It certainly makes a defense think as it is forced to adjust its fronts, secondary run supports, coverages, and perhaps its stunts and blitzes to an unbalanced formation. In addition, unbalanced formation problems for the defense can be magnified by using differing personnel plans, alignment sets (wings, off set backs), shifts, and motions. Diagram 14-1 shows an unbalanced formation that leaves an eligible tight end to the backside. Diagram 14-2 shows an unbalanced formation created by a backside tight end shift and motion action with a one-back set.

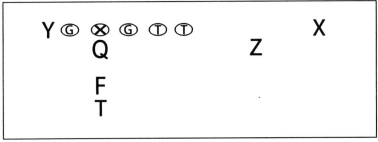

Diagram 14-1. Unbalanced formation with eligible backside tight end

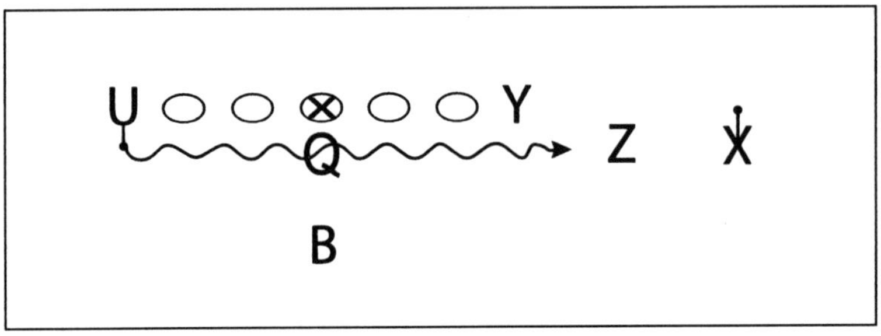

Diagram 14-2. Backside tight end shift and motion to create a one-back unbalanced formation

Concept #15: Defenses do not like to see bunched formations.

Defenses do not like to see bunched offensive formations. The design of bunched offensive formations makes excellent use of the expansion-contraction theory of attacking defenses, which will be discussed later in this book. In this theory, offenses contract, or tighten, their offensive formation and sets to aid outside breaking runs and passes. By contacting a formation, the offense contracts the defense covering the formation helping in the efforts to outflank it. The bunch action is, of course, contraction action.

Bunch formations are a multiple formation distraction to defenses. The defense must now adjust its fronts, secondary run supports, coverages, and (possibly) stunts and blitzes—at least to the bunch formation side. One of the disturbing factors for the defense is that a good chance exists that secondary defenders will have to be brought down in alignment to play unnatural alignments and techniques on the bunched offenders. Coverages, such as cover 2, are often heavily disturbed by the alignment adjustments they must make to a bunched formation. In addition, it is very easy to magnify the problems a bunched formation presents to a defense by utilizing varying personnel plans, shifts, and motions. Additionally, an offense can actually bunch its receivers to both sides. Diagram 15-1 shows a bunched formation from a two-tight-end, one-back personnel plan with return motion action.

Bunched plays are not limited to passes. Diagram 15-2 shows a bunch formation quick toss run play to the bunch formation. In addition, if the defense overloads to the bunch formation side, runs and passes away from the bunch formation can be very effective.

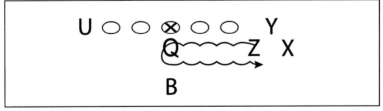

Diagram 15-1. Bunched formation from a two-tight-end, one-back personnel plan with return motion action

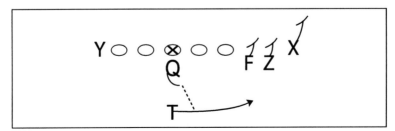

Diagram 15-2. Quick toss play to bunch formation

Concept #16: Defenses do not like to see empty formations.

Many defensive coaches do not like the new offensive trend of wide open, spread out, passing football. If that is true, then those defensive coaches would most dislike the empty passing game. For the most part, empty formation football spreads a defense out maximally from sideline to sideline. Five receivers, up close to the line of scrimmage, present a variety of horizontal and vertical pass threats for the defense to contend with. And in spreading the defense so thinly in coverage, the defense can become extremely susceptible to quarterback runs, especially the quarterback draw.

Using no backs/empty formations does much to heighten and magnify the concept of multiple offensive football. How does the defense react and align to a no backs/empty formation? What about when varied personnel plans are utilized to create no backs/empty formations? And, what about shifts and motions? All of these thoughts help the offense to attack the defense. They help to keep a defense sitting back on their heels being more concerned with adjustments than reading and reacting. And, as has been already been shown in Diagram 10-1, irregular usage of a specific personnel plan (no backs/empty from pro set personnel) further helps to distract and attack a defense. Diagram 16-1 shows a five-wide-receiver personnel plan, no backs/empty formation with across the formation motion.

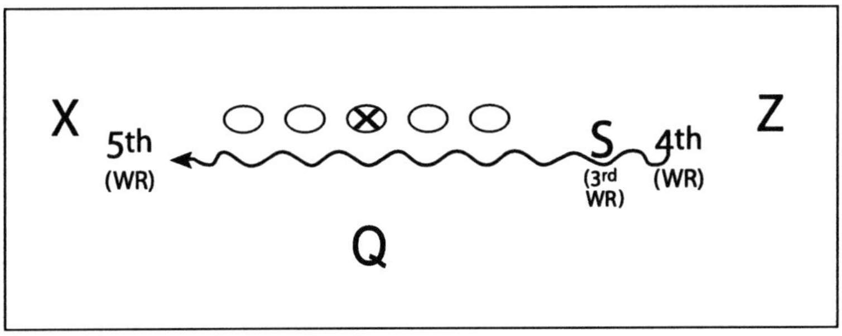

Diagram 16-1. Empty formation with a five-wide-receiver personnel plan with cross motion

Concept #17: Not being multiple helps for offensive simplicity and clarity.

To this point in the book, much has been said about using multiple offense concepts to attack defenses and help produce effective offense. This author is a proponent of multiple offensive usage in an effort to make a defense react to the offense rather than the opposite occurring—to *attack* rather than to *be* attacked. However, much is to be said for not utilizing a multiple offense approach.

Many coaches primarily use a pro set formation and rarely vary their formations, personnel plans or utilize shifting and motioning concepts. And, many do it quite effectively. Yes, defenses may draw up their playbooks and create their defensive designs against right and left pro set formations. However, conservatively utilizing one, or a few, basic formations—and not utilizing a more multiple offense approach—has distinct advantages.

Using one, or a few, basic formations allows an offense to operate in a more settled, declared mode. The defense may have a reasonably clear (and better) idea of what the offense may be attempting to do. However, the offense will also have the ability to quickly see what the defense is going to do to try to stop the offense. In addition, it is often easier for an offense to make adjustments to what a defense is trying to do when a smaller, more compact, non-multiple offensive approach is utilized. A limited amount of formations, personnel plans, shifts, and motions helps to allow for a greater ability of the offensive players to focus on a more limited amount of adjustment needs rather than the larger volume of adjustment needs a multiple offensive approach might necessitate. Much of this thinking goes back to the "Keep It Simple, Stupid" (KISS) concept. The tighter and smaller the offensive package used, the greater the ability for an offense to focus on execution. More (multiplicity) may not necessarily mean better.

Concept #18: Use expansion and contraction theory of formationing.

In the expansion and contraction theory of formationing, offenses expand or contract their offensive formations to aid in or out breaking runs, pass routes and pass patterns. If the run or pass action is to the inside, the formation action is to expand or widen. In this fashion, the defense is expanded and widened, or spread out, in an effort to aid in breaking runs and passes. Diagram 18-1 shows the use of an expanded, spread out, widened formation for an in-breaking double-slant pass pattern.

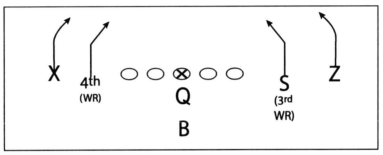

Diagram 18-1. Spread formation for in breaking double slant pass pattern

If the run or pass action is to the outside, the formation action is to contract or tighten. In this fashion, the defense is contracted and tightened to aid out breaking runs and passes. The contracted formation helps to contract the defensive alignments helping to make it easier for the defense to be out flanked. Diagram 18-2 shows a contracted, tightened formation for a sweep run play. Diagram 18-3 shows the use of a contracted, tightened formation for a flood play-action pass pattern.

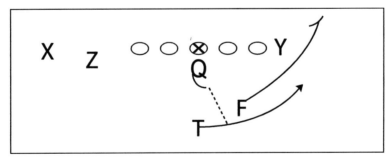

Diagram 18-2. Tightened formation for outside sweep run action

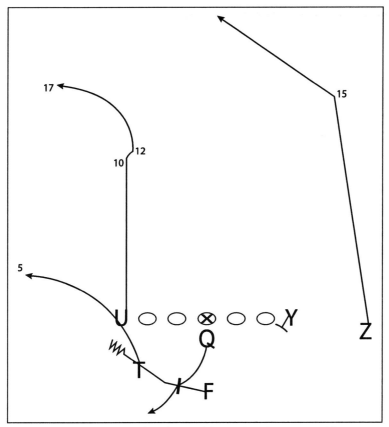

Diagram 18-3. Contracted, tightened formation for an outside breaking flood play-action pass pattern

Concept #19: Use the horizontal width of the field in both the run and the passing games.

As an offense moves the football across midfield, it starts to be effected by vertical shrinkage of the field. This becomes increasingly true as an offense moves into the red zone and goal line areas. However, what always remains constant is the fact that from goal line to goal line, the horizontal distance of the football *never* changes. As a result, the offense must be sure to make maximal use of the constant horizontal sideline-to-sideline distance through the use of the expansion and contraction theory.

Use the constant horizontal width of the field to expand the defense with widened, spread out formations for inside breaking runs such as draws, traps, and dives and passes such as digs, square-ins, curls, and drags. Such a widened formational usage helps spread out the front and coverage. It forces each defender to have more lateral, or horizontal, territory to defend in its efforts to defend against inside runs and pass routes. Such wide splitting must, however, be disguised whenever possible. A good time to disguise such wide splitting is when the football is being run or thrown out wide to the opposite side. Diagram 19-1 shows the use of a maximally split, spread formation to spread out the defense for an inside breaking double square-in pass pattern.

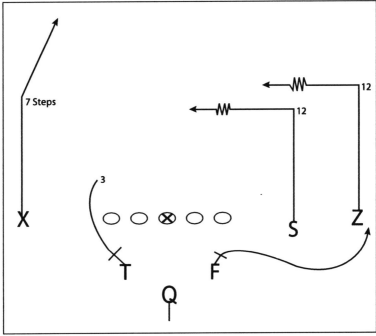

Diagram 19-1. Spread formation to spread defense for inside breaking square-in routes

Tightened splits and tightened formations are used to influence a defense to aid outside breaking routes, patterns, and runs. In this case, outside runs (such as sweeps, zone stretches, options, and bounces) and out-breaking-type routes and patterns (such as outs, post-corners, flats, swings, and outside flood route pattern combinations) are aided by using compacted formations and tightened alignments by the receivers. Such tightened formations and wide receiver splits help to compact (or tighten) the defense making it more difficult to defend against outside runs and out breaking routes and patterns. The tightening/compacting aspect gives such runs and routes more room, or space, to work into, and it gives the offense a better chance to outflank the defenders who are positioned tightly to the inside. Diagram 19-2 shows the use of a tightened pro set formation via the use of return flanker motion to compact the coverage and set up an out route throw.

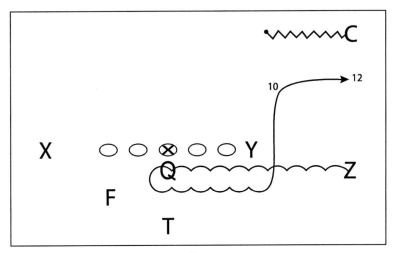

Diagram 19-2. Motioning to condense a coverage to set up an out route throw

Concept #20: Be sure to attack the upfield, vertical distance of the field with the passing game.

The vertical distance of the football does get affected once it closes in on the red zone and goal line. However, no matter how close the offense is to the goal line, it must stretch the defense vertically as much as it can. If a defense is experiencing little or no vertical threat, the defense is then able to sit down on the offense with its secondary. Such shortened depth, secondary defender alignments are able to sit on top of intermediate depth pass routes to a greater degree. In addition, such secondary defenders are also up tighter in a better alignment to act as run support defenders. The bottom line is that an offense *must* threaten a defense deep with its passing game.

Offenses must throw the football deep with its passing game to threaten the secondary. No secondary wants the football thrown over its head, thereby giving up big play yardage and a possible touchdown. Once a deep-pass threat is established, a secondary is going to be much less willing to sit down on intermediate pass routes or cheat up to be in a better position to support the run. And, throwing deep does not just mean streak routes. Completing a post-corner, an out-and-up, or a post route will all help to produce deep yardage throwing gains. It will help "blow-the-top" off of the coverage.

However, one important thought to this concep is that deep passes are not thrown just to threaten a defense deep. They are thrown to get completions deep, which will threaten a defense deep. Deep passes are not to be thought of as wasted plays just to influence the defense to stay deep. Diagram 20-1 shows a maximal vertical attack of a shortened red zone vertical area in an effort to still threaten a defense vertically as best possible.

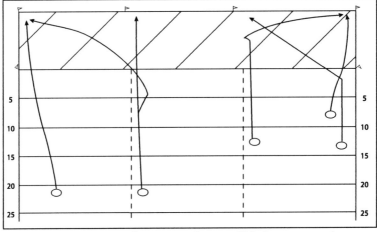

Diagram 20-1. Deep red zone passing to still help create as best a vertical stretch on the defense as possible

Concept #21: Be sure to account for hash mark and middle-of-the-field considerations.

An offense must be sure to account for hash mark and middle-of-the-field considerations in both game-plan formulation and in the analysis of your opposition's defensive structure. Certain offensive plays are hindered (or helped) by having the football on the hash. Is an out pass to the field too far to expect an accurate throw from your quarterback when the football is on the hash? Is there enough room to run a run option play into the boundary when the football is on the hash? Some runs and passes need, or are greatly helped by, the extra room afforded to the field when the football is on the hash.

When the football is in the middle of the field, weakside split end side plays are afforded more room to operate as the formation side plays can become slightly more congested. In addition, your hash mark and middle-of-the-field analysis of the opponent's defense may show that it is a heavy stunt/blitz pressure defense when on the hash marks but basic and conservative when in the middle of the field. Or, a defense may show that it always plays cover 2 when the football is on the hash and cover 3 when in the middle of the field. Such considerations should importantly impact your game plans and play.

Concept #22: Attack the perimeter.

One of the most devastating situations for a defense is to have an offense get the football to the outside after having broken the defense's perimeter contain efforts. Once the offense does break through and gets the football to the outside, little defense is left to stop the offense. While little defense is left, plenty of "green grass" is available for the ballcarrier to work into. Breaking defensive containment means that the offense is outside the defense's central core—the thickness of the defense. In addition, the offense is running (or passing) away from the backside rush and pursuit.

In theory, all of this makes good, practical sense. Unfortunately, many offenses don't do a good job of attacking the perimeter when it certainly should. An offense can get on the corner in a number of ways; the sweep, toss, or quick pitch game quickly comes to mind, as does the outside zone stretch play. The run option game is designed to get the football on the perimeter. The same is true for moving pass pocket actions such as roll-out and sprint-out actions. Bubble screens, wide receiver screens, and basic flare screens can effectively help attack the perimeter. To have an effective offense, being a strong perimeter run and pass team must be a priority. Saying "We just can't get outside" is not acceptable. Diagram 22-1 shows a trap option play to help get the football on the perimeter.

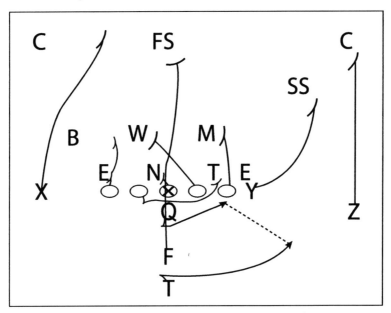

Diagram 22-1. Trap option play to get the football on the perimeter

Concept #23: Great offenses run the football.

Great football teams run the football. They can efficiently run the football on par downs (first and ten, second and medium or less) as well as on key, critical offensive situations such as coming-out offense, third and short offense, and on the goal line. It is hard to develop a physical team if you don't run the football. Not having a tough, hard-nosed run game can greatly affect your defense in a negative fashion. Your defense is going to have to stop other hard-nosed, tough offenses to help your team win. Your offense is the offense your defense will practice against each day in some form. If your defense practices against a weak run game, its chance of developing into a good run defense will be hindered.

At times your team is going to have to run the football to be able to win. As a result, you better make sure that you can run the football. Team toughness and team morale go hand in hand. One of the best ways to establish a tough, hard-nosed attitude is through the physicality of being a good run team. In addition, when an offense can effectively run the football, passing becomes a lot easier.

Concept #24: Explosive offensive line get-off and low pad level is the foundation of effective run blocking.

If you want to develop a good run game, explosive offensive line get-off and low pad level is a must. Both are the base and foundation of good offensive line blocking. Exploding off the ball on the variety of snap counts that an offense may use must be drilled and practiced until the entire offensive line can explode off the line of scrimmage as one. The linemen must come off the ball with low, flat backs to enable them to deliver their blocks with proper pad control up under the pads of the defense. The linemen must then be taught to explosively punch their blocks (hands) into the chest cavity of the defenders in front of them so the blockers are controlling the defenders rather than having the opposite occur.

The coaches should be sure that the linemen are keeping their eyes on the actual contact of the hands of the blockers into the chest cavity of the defenders. A common fault of many blockers is to close their eyes as contact is made causing misplacement of the hands. The key, however, is still pad level. Whoever has proper pad level at the line of scrimmage almost always wins the line of scrimmage battle.

Concept #25: Use run designs that have varied timings.

Run plays have designs that can vary tremendously in timing. A misdirection cross buck with backside pulling linemen leading the way can vary in timing tremendously from its complementary inside dive. The same is true for a slow developing sprint draw play and a quick developing trap. In between the timing of both the slow developing plays and quick hitters are intermediately time runs plays such as isolations, blasts, and powers. Such a mixture of run play timings is an effective way of helping to throw off the timing of the defense as it tries to defense all three different run play timings.

Defense is very rhythmic, which is especially true in the defensive front where linebackers work hard to pace the flow of a run play so that gaps are filled at the right time with cut back lanes well protected. As a result, defenses like offensive run games that have run timings that are similar: all quick, all slow, or, all in between. Making it difficult for the defense to pace runs that are well mixed in their timings requires greater discipline by the defense in regard to patience and properly pacing the timing of the run at hand.

Diagrams 25-1 through 25-3 show run plays with varied timings. Diagram 25-1 shows a quick hitting trap play. Diagram 25-2 shows an intermediately time draw play. Diagram 25-3 shows a slow developing sprint draw play.

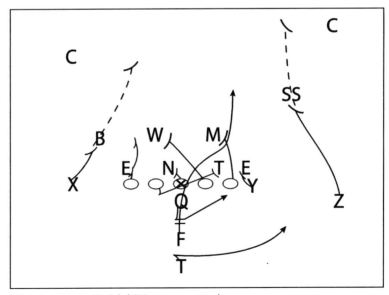

Diagram 25-1. Quick hitting trap run play

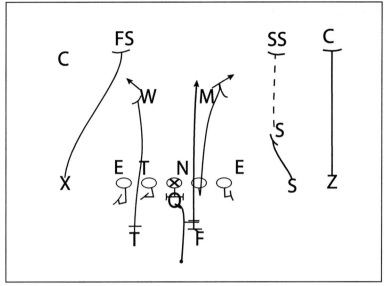

Diagram 25-2. Intermediately timed draw run play

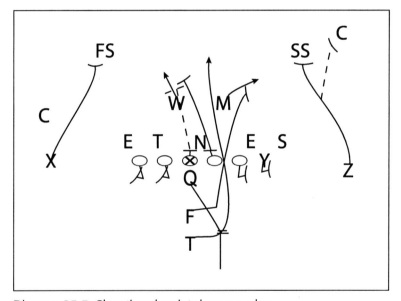

Diagram 25-3. Slow timed sprint draw run play

Concept #26: Use only enough base runs.

Your base run package should be a tightly knit run design of two to three (possibly four) base, bread-and-butter runs. All other runs that are a part of the base package should be complementary runs that help to balance the attack of the entire run package.

What should be the total number of runs in such a tight, base run package? Five runs? Six? Maybe seven? (Seven really starts to stretch it.) Certainly not 11 or 12 base runs. Some one-back zone teams utilize an inside and an outside zone run play, a counter, and a draw play—and that's it. Why? Because what's really important is that the number of run plays in your base run package should be an amount that can be practiced to perfection. It is not how many different types of runs that you have in your arsenal to use. It's how many runs you have that you can teach and practice so that they can be run consistently and effectively versus the wide variety of defensive looks they may see.

Concept #27: Zone run blocking schemes can be very forgiving.

Zone run blocking is very forgiving. Zone blocked run plays can be very effective in handling a multitude of defensive stunt and blitz variety. Zone run blocking allows the blockers to pick up the defenders that enter their run block zones—be they defensive linemen, linebackers, or blitzing defensive backs. As a result, such zone blocking can help to best pick up cross charge type twists and stunts.

Zone blocking allows for the blockers to come off the line of scrimmage aggressively and assuredly, able to focus on the stepping to and the blocking of their zone rather than a specific defender and his possible multitude of movement actions. Diagram 27-1 shows a zone blocked onside zone stretch run play to combat stunt pressure.

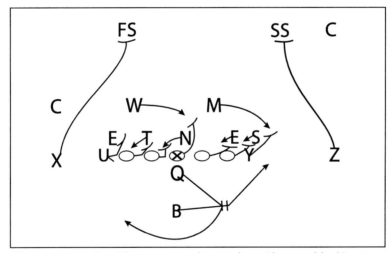

Diagram 27-1. Outside zone stretch run play with zone blocking to pick up stunt pressure

Concept #28: Base run blocking schemes can often best pick up stunt and blitz pressures.

If a defense is stunt and blitz oriented, base-blocked run plays can help ensure the blocking of each stunt and blitz with man-to-man blocked schemes. Base, man-blocked plays are the simplest means of "covering up" the stunt/blitz defenders and eliminating penetration with the least amount of confusion. Since much stunt/blitz design relies on creating confusion, base-blocked run plays help in eliminating uncertainty. If all of the pressuring stunt/blitz defenders are simply covered up, the ballcarrier has a tremendous chance to pop through the line of scrimmage to produce a big gain. This result is often true because very little defense is usually left behind with such stunt/blitz action—especially if some type of man coverage is being utilized in conjunction with the stunt or blitz.

Base blocked schemes enable "hat-on-hat" block approaches to handling a multitude of defensive stunt/blitz varieties, which greatly helps to prevent the "turning loose" of stunting or blitzing defenders. In addition, base, man-to-man blocking is an excellent alternate blocking scheme to go to if the defensive linemen grab onto—or even tackle—zone blockers in their zone blocking efforts. Diagram 28-1 shows the use of a base-blocked isolation type play to combat defenses that like to stunt and blitz.

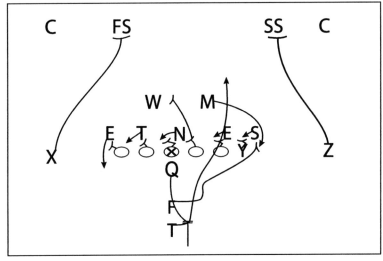

Diagram 28-1. Base blocked isolation play to combat defensive stunt and blitz pressure

Concept #29: Quick-hitting run plays help keep defenses honest.

Quick-hitting run plays can definitely help keep defenses honest. Dives, traps, and belly plays can quickly crease defensive fronts that have fast flowing linebackers and angling or slanting defensive linemen. In addition, quick-hitting plays can take advantage of penetrating fronts and hard, upfield pass rushers. Whether by trap action, double-teams at the point of attack, zone blocking, or one-on-one man blocking, a quick hitting run play can pop into the secondary for large gains. Diagram 29-1 shows a zone-blocked inside zone run play with a double-team movement block at the point of attack.

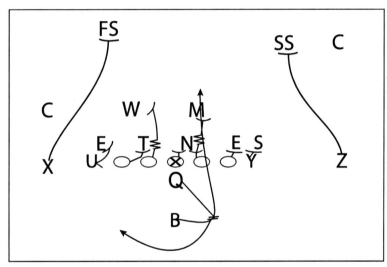

Diagram 29-1. Inside zone run play with double-team movement block at the point of attack

Concept #30: Trapping can greatly attack penetrating defenses.

Traps can effectively attack upfield, penetrating defenders. Such penetrating defenders actually make themselves vulnerable to backside gap seal block action and the actual trap block. While this develops, blocking paths are actually cleared to the linebackers for the second level linebacker blockers. Diagram 30-1 shows a trap-blocking scheme versus a penetrating, pass rushing 4-3 defense.

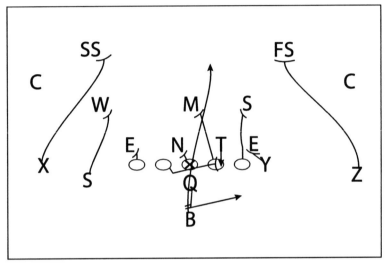

Diagram 30-1. Trap play vs. penetrating 4-3 defense

Concept #31: Draws are important run support pieces for an effective pass offense.

Amidst today's wide open, highly effective pass offenses, the draw play is an extremely important support run play. It is an excellent way to slow down heavy pass rush efforts. The draw is the one run play that directly complements the passing game.

Draw plays are often executed off of a team's base pass protection scheme. The pass blockers set and sell pass protection, then aggressively take on their penetrating pass rushers and block them in the direction they want to go. The tackles inside set to invite an outside rush by the end line of pass rushers to help give the draw ballcarrier inside run lanes. Any inside uncovered line blockers work up to block the linebackers after a short delay to allow the linebackers to get into their pass drops. The draw ballcarrier usually makes his break off of the block of the first covered lineman from the center to the playside. A base blocked draw is shown in Diagram 31-1 versus a 4-2 nickel defense.

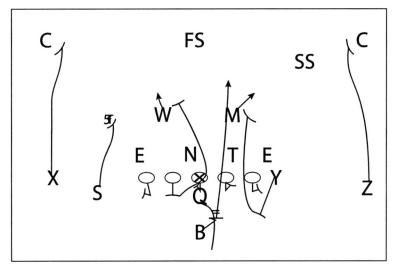

Diagram 31-1. Base blocked draw vs. 4-2 nickel defense

Concept #32: Quarterback draws can be extremely effective.

Quarterback draws can often give offenses an extra man advantage versus defenses. Versus certain man coverage schemes, the quarterback is the one ballcarrier who is not well covered by the defense. With the use of spread formations and motioning, an offense can thin out the defense horizontally, leaving little defense left to cover a quarterback draw. Such draw action can be very effective even if the quarterback is not an exceptionally good runner. By thinning (or spreading out) the defense, the blockers are afforded excellent blocking angles to clear an easy run path for the quarterback. As a result, quarterback draws can help exploit a spread out 4-1 man coverage dime defense as shown in Diagram 32-1.

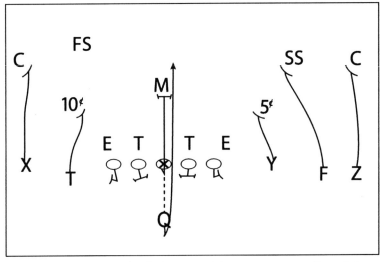

Diagram 32-1. Quarterback draw vs. 4-1 man coverage dime defense

Concept #33: Misdirection runs are a must.

Misdirection offense is a must. Misdirection runs need to be an intrinsic part of any offense's misdirection design. Defenses are built around pursuit to the football. If an offensive design doesn't have effective misdirection runs, little help may be available to slow down a defense that "flies" to the football. Conversely, a defense that pursues hard to the football leaves itself vulnerable to misdirection runs. Diagram 33-1 shows an I misdirection counter run play versus a fast pursuing reduced Eagle defensive front.

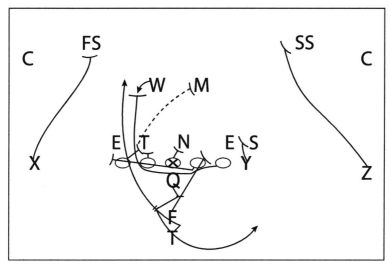

Diagram 33-1. I formation misdirection counter vs. reduced Eagle defense

Concept #34: Slow-developing and/or pulling-linemen run plays can be disturbed by stunt/blitz pressure.

Slow-developing plays often fall prey to attacking, pressuring defenses. You do not want to see a heavy penetrating defense against a slow-developing counter- or cross-buck-type play in which frontside blockers down seal block to the inside and the backside guard and tackle pull to kick out block and lead block up on a linebacker. Defensive action that blows gaps and pressures heavily upfield can easily disturb and dismantle such a blocking scheme. A single penetrator bursting through the line of scrimmage can easily pick off such pulling linemen, rendering their blocking actions useless. As a result, simple base- and zone-blocked run plays may be better able to target and block the multiple, penetrating stunts/blitzes schemes that a defense may present. Diagram 34-1 shows how penetration can disturb a slow developing "I" counter misdirection run play.

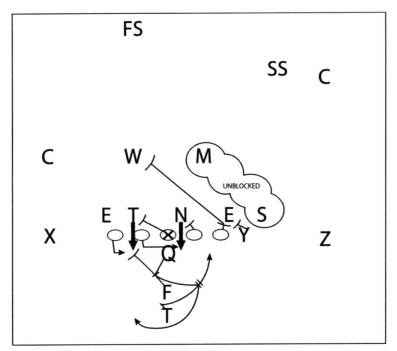

Diagram 34-1. Penetrating defenders disturbing a slow developing "I" counter misdirection run play

Concept #35: Offenses who are good at shutting off penetration use slow developing and/or pulling linemen run plays effectively.

A wing-T-type offense that utilizes a cross buck or counter play as a base part of their offense may feel confident that such a misdirection play is, very much, a bread and butter type play of its offense. For them, the cross-buck or counter is a play to be used in any field position from goal line to goal line. No matter what type of slower offensive play being used, the key factor is whether or not the offense can execute the play properly versus the problems presented by a stunting/blitzing and penetrating defense. If an offense is proficient in sealing a wide variety of defensive stunts and blitzes to the inside, and can consistently shut off penetration on the line of scrimmage, it should not fear running a sprint draw, cross-buck, counter, or any other slow developing type of play, pulling backside linemen or not. This statement is especially true if the play is a base play in the offense and the offensive players have confidence that they know (and can execute) the play well. Diagram 35-1 shows a slow developing "I" counter misdirection run play that effectively shuts off an inside penetrating stunt.

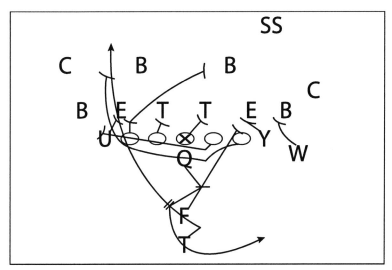

Diagram 35-1. Slow developing "I" counter misdirection run play effectively shutting off goal line penetration

Concept #36: Defenses hate run option football.

Defenses hate to face run option football teams. Run option football forces defenses to be assignment oriented. Versus triple option play possibilities, the defense is forced to assign at least one defender to the inside run fake, one to the quarterback and one to the pitch back. The defense is now limited in its ability to "fly" to the football as it might normally do when faced with non-option-type run plays. Every front, coverage, stunt, and blitz utilized by the defense must be sure to assign a defender to the inside run (dive, belly, trap) threat, the quarterback's keep option, or the running back's pitch option.

The amazing factor involved with running some form of run option football is how disturbing run option football is to a defense due to the need to be assignment oriented. As a result, many defenses cut back significantly when facing run option teams, fearing the need for strict option phase assignments on each and every front, coverage, stunt, and blitz utilized. An offense doesn't need to be a strict run option team to force such results. Knowing that an offense runs from eight to ten options per game will often be enough to force a defense to become option assignment oriented and limit their total defensive volume as a result. Diagram 36-1 shows how a 3-4 Okie front is forced to be option oriented versus an I triple option offense.

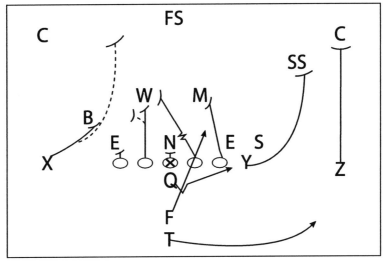

Diagram 36-1. I triple option vs. 3-4 Okie front defense

Concept #37: Run options can be very effective versus man (blitz) coverages.

Run options can be extremely effective versus man coverage defenses, whether the man coverage is tied into stunts and blitzes or not. If the defense is stunt/blitz oriented, certain options like the speed and lead options can be particularly effective. This situation can be true if stunts and blitzes are inside (or outside) oriented. The offense is able to quickly seal inside stunts off to the inside as the offense options to the outside. If the stunt or blitz comes from the outside, zone reach scoop blocking allows the offense to isolate the end of line keep-pitch option key quickly for potential big games. In addition, if it is known that the coverage is going to be some form of man coverage, the offense can formation and/or motion the man coverage to overload to one side as it options away to the other side.

Diagram 37-1 shows a speed option play sealing off an inside blitz to get to the outside. The formation and motion action influences the man coverage strength away from the option action.

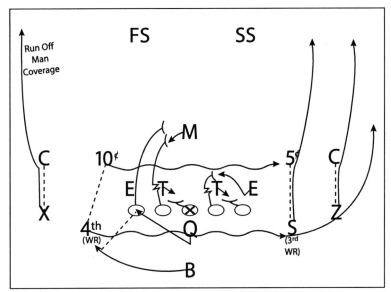

Diagram 37-1. Speed option play sealing off inside stunt/blitz as motion takes man coverage away from option action

Concept #38: Options help to neutralize eight-man fronts.

Run options are often an excellent answer to defenses that utilize eight-man fronts. Versus an eight-man front, it's hard to account for the fourth defender (from inside-out) on both sides of the ball in regard to blocking schemes. This situation may be especially true to the split end side (in a pro set formation away from the formation strength side) since the offense has one less blocker. Run option plays help account for this extra defender since the quarterback now becomes a "one more player" threat for the defense to contend with. Diagram 38-1 shows how a lead option play strong to the formation side helps account for an eight-man front's four-defender strong problem.

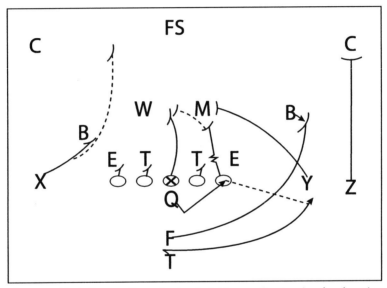

Diagram 38-1. Run option attack of eight-man front using lead option

Concept #39: Shotgun option football explosively ties together triple option football with shotgun pass action.

One of the criticisms of using the shotgun formation has been the relatively limited effective run game that can be executed from the shotgun set. This criticism has been true until recently. The use of shotgun triple option offense has dynamically tied together two explosive offensive elements—the shotgun and the triple option. Now, defenses can no longer just lock in on a shotgun offense's passing game; they must be as equally concerned about being assignment oriented versus the three phases of the triple option, the inside zone run, the quarterback's keep option, and the running back's pitch option. Add to this the shovel pass with its triple option design and you have two extremely effective triple option designs that can be executed from the shotgun.

Diagram 39-1 shows the shotgun triple option play versus a reduced Eagle defense. Diagram 39-2 shows the shotgun shovel pass triple option play versus a reduced Eagle defense.

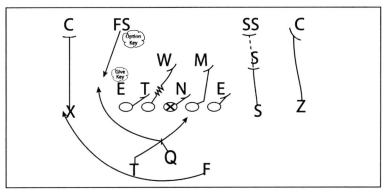

Diagram 39-1. Shotgun triple option action vs. reduced Eagle defense

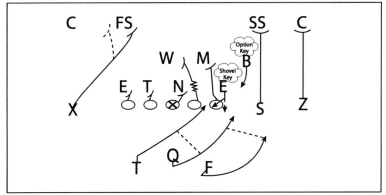

Diagram 39-2. Shotgun shovel pass triple option action vs. reduced Eagle defense

Concept #40: Backfield faking is often one of the most overlooked/under-coached offensive techniques.

Most coaches would quickly agree to the importance of good backfield ball faking. Sucking up linebackers on a run fake and throwing to a dig route over the linebackers' heads because they are out of position to effectively cover the route points to the importance of run faking. The same may be true on a cross-buck type misdirection action in which a good fake to a dive back may be just enough to eliminate the pursuit of a linebacker in getting to the course of the offside counter back. Or, the fake may be just what is needed to set up a seal block on a linebacker on the same cross-buck counter misdirection action. Good ball faking can pay excellent dividends to the help in the execution of run and play-action pass plays.

One of the problems with the development of good ball faking skills is that the skill is often given little attention by coaches. Ball faking skills need to be taught, coached, and practiced like any other offensive football skill. The more the quality coaching attention the skill receives, the greater your players' ball faking skills will be.

A fun drill to use to help develop proper ball faking skills is the "Fool the Coach" drill. In this drill, the coach stands in front of a backfield set. He then calls out a series to be executed. "Counter" might be the call. The quarterback then whispers to the backfield one of the plays associated with that series to be executed—the dive, counter, or bootleg. The players then proceed to execute the play called with as precise a ball faking skills as possible. The coach scores each play ("Good job, a nine," or, "Just fair, a seven." Even better is to have a videographer taking video of the action from right in front of the backfield action set up at linebacker depth. Watching such training video quickly helps the quarterback and running backs to understand just how important ball faking is. Diagram 40-1 shows the "Fool the Coach" backfield faking drill.

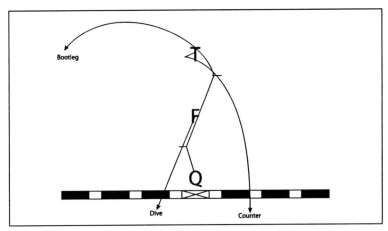

Diagram 40-1. "Fool the Coach" backfield faking drill

Concept #41: Wide receiver run blocking can be the big difference maker.

Whenever you coach wide receivers, one of the first statements you should make to them at the first practice of the year is: "If you don't block, you don't play." That may seem to be a strong statement. However, if you were to carefully watch a football game at *any* level, one of the first thing you would notice is that wide receiver run blocking is often the weak link of the offense's efforts to block. How often do you see a back break into the secondary only to see a poor block, or even a "whiff," by a wide receiver lead to only a moderate gain. When wide receivers are blocking downfield effectively, good things happen. The ballcarriers are running for huge gains or taking it to the end zone for six.

Wide receiver blocking is an attitude. If your wide receivers are helped to understand the importance of their blocking roles, they can be a tremendous factor in the total effectiveness of the offense's run game. And, good downfield wide receiver run blocking skills can be easily transformed into good downfield wide receiver blocking skills on pass plays to block for another receiver who has caught the football. Wide receiver blocking needs toughness, grit, and proper coaching attention. It is an important skill that must be taught, coached, and practiced vitally. In practice, running downfield and playing two-handed touch with a scout squad player will not do it. Bursting off the ball, taking a proper block approach course, breaking down on the defender as the receiver begins to step on his toes, looking the block punch in, and pressing the bock until the whistle blows will.

An excellent drill to use to help develop good wide receiver run blocking is the 11-on-9 run and play-action drill shown in Diagram 41-1. The drill is, simply, a 9-on-9 run drill versus the defense with the wide receivers added to the drill to block the safety, or safeties. Play-action passes are sprinkled in to the drill to keep the defense honest in regard to run support. In addition, the drill gives the offense a chance to develop its play-action passing game under pressure.

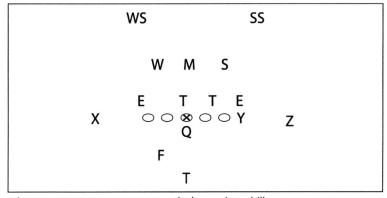

Diagram 41-1. 11-on-9 run and play-action drill

Concept #42: Crackback blocking greatly disturbs the play of linebackers.

Linebackers are often the quarterbacks of the defense. They are often the defensive leaders. They play in the front, "down and dirty" with the defensive linemen. On a pass play, they drop back to pass cover with the defensive backs if they're not involved in a stunt or blitz. From their covered up alignments (defensive linemen cover up offensive linemen making it hard for offensive linemen to block linebackers), they are often expected to be the first to the football to make tackles.

One of the best ways to disturb the play of linebackers is to crackback block them. Linebackers are usually well schooled in taking on the blocks of offensive linemen and running backs. However, taking on a delayed crackback block by a wide receiver or a flexed tight end is a different story. Physical crackback blocking can greatly disturb the reading and reacting action of a linebacker. And once linebackers know that there is a crackback threat, they are given one more offensive threat to have to worry about. Diagram 42-1 shows split end crackback blocking on a lead option play.

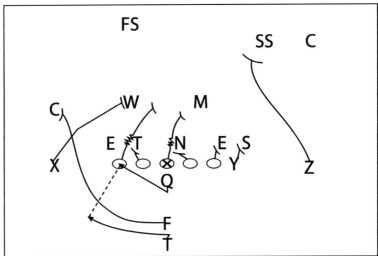

Diagram 42-1. Split end crackback blocking on a lead option play

Concept #43: Have a limited amount of base pass patterns that can be applied in a variety of ways.

Much like putting together a base run game design, a base pass pattern design should be made up of a tight, limited number of pass patterns. A maximum of 10 to 12 patterns is about the right number to utilize in a pass attack. Some coaches who have excellent pass attacks use even less; any more risks having too much passing game. Just like the run game, it's not necessarily how *much* you do in the passing game, but how *well* you do what you do. The more passing game you have, the less chance your players will have to learn to execute the greater volume of pass offense properly versus the large variety of pass coverage schemes they may see.

The pass patterns should complement one another in regard to what each pattern is trying to accomplish. Some of the pass patterns should be zone beaters. Some should be more oriented to beating man-to-man coverages. Some should specifically attack two-deep safety coverages. Others should be designed to attack single safety coverages. A key, however, is to be able to apply your base pass patterns in a variety of ways in regard to varied formations, personnel plans, shifts, and motions. In this fashion, a defense can face a wide variety of pass offense if a coach wants to be multiple in his approach. In reality, the pass offense is executing a limited number of pass plays. It is just applying those base pass patterns over and over in a variety of ways.

Diagram 43-1 shows a cross pattern from a three-wide-receiver personnel plan balanced doubles formation. Diagram 43-2 shows the same cross pass pattern being applied from a two-tight, one-back, two-wide receiver personnel plan and formation.

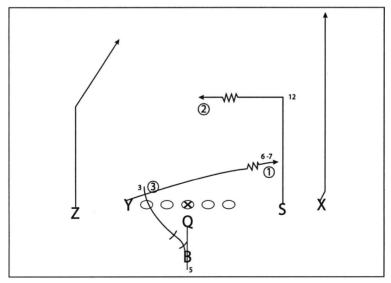

Diagram 43-1. Cross pattern from a three-wide-receiver, one-back personnel plan doubles formation

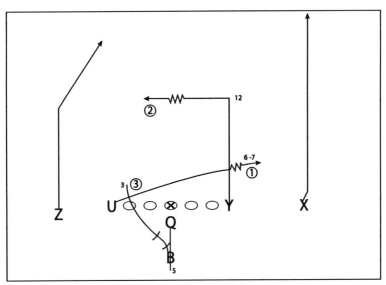

Diagram 43-2. Cross pattern from a two-tight-end, one-back, two-wide-receiver personnel plan and formation

Diagram 43-3 shows the same cross pass pattern from a pro personnel plan twins formation with tailback motion to a flanker position. All three diagrams show the same pass pattern, all read by the quarterback in the same way. The cross pattern is simply applied differently with personnel, formation, motion, and shift variation.

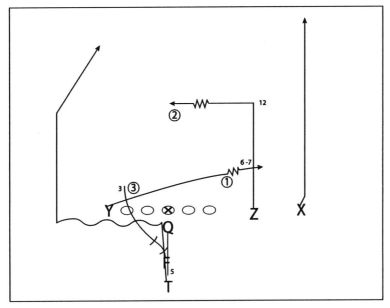

Diagram 43-3. Cross pattern from a pro personnel plan twins formation with tailback motion

Concept #44: The sum of your pass patterns and their routes should attack the entire field both horizontally and vertically.

In Concept #43, it was stated that your base pass patterns should complement one another in regard to what each pattern is trying to accomplish. Where this is most necessary is in the horizontal and vertical attack of the field in relation to the routes of the base patterns. Do your base patterns attack all of the deep passing zones? Do they attack all of the short and intermediate passing zones from sideline to sideline? If they do not, then savvy opposing coaches will void the coverages of such areas of the field and overload the ones you do attack.

Plot your patterns on a sheet of paper. Place one pattern drawing on top of the previous until all of your base patterns are shown on top of one another. Are there zones that the routes of your pass patterns do not attack? If so, it may be time to redesign your base pass patterns. Another (and perhaps easier) way to examine the overall route distribution attack of the sum of your patterns is to use overlays and an overhead projector. Simply lay overlays of your base patterns on top of one another to analyze your overall base pass pattern route distributions.

Concept #45: Dropback passing game routes and patterns must time with the steps and drop depth of your quarterback.

It is very important to make sure that the quarterback drop step timing and quarterback drop depth on a pass pattern times with the depth and timing of the pass routes being run. As a result, if the quarterback's dropback pass step timing is a three-step drop, the pass pattern routes utilized should be quick passing game routes. The quarterback should then be throwing to hitches, slants, quick speed-outs, and fade-type routes as shown in Diagram 45-1.

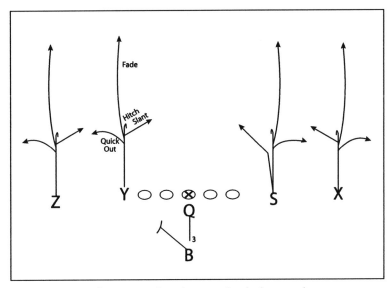

Diagram 45-1. Three-step timed quarterback drop and routes

Diagram 45-2 shows a five-step timed drop by the quarterback. A five-step drop times with intermediate depth routes such as outs, square-ins, and curls. Highly timed five-step drop streak routes also time to a five-step timed drop by the quarterback.

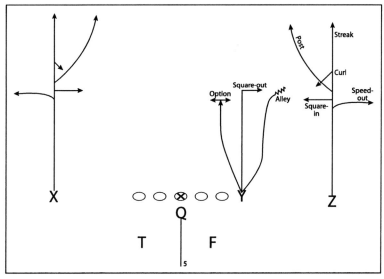

Diagram 45-2. Five-step timed quarterback drop and routes

Diagram 45-3 shows a seven-step timed drop by the quarterback. A seven-step drop times with deeper, slower developing routes such as digs, deep hooks, and comeback-outs.

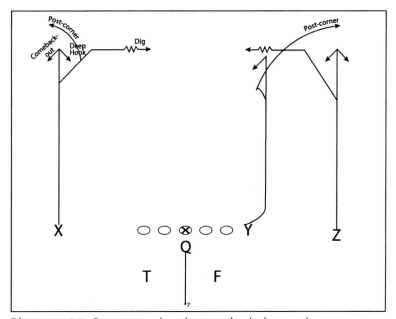

Diagram 45-3. Seven-step timed quarterback drop and routes

Concept #46: If you want to have an effective passing game, avoid seven-step drop timed throwing.

If a coach wants to have an effective passing offense, he should base his pass design on three- and five-step timed quarterback drop pass routes. Conversely, the more a pass design is built around delayed, seven-step timed pass routes, the greater the chances for passing failure. The reason for this stems from pass protection ability.

The bottom line is that the longer a pass protection has to hold up to enable the quarterback to successfully deliver his pass, the less the chance for success. Pass protection is not easy. Five or six blockers may execute their block techniques excellently. However, if one blocker breaks down, it may very well lead to a sack or quarterback pressure. The same can be true for three- and five-step timed passing, you say? That certainly can be true. However, a direct correlation exists between pass protection success and the length of time needed for the quarterback to successfully deliver a pass. Simply, it is a lot easier to protect for quicker, highly timed three- and five-step timed passing than it is for delayed, seven-step timed passing.

Concept #47: Throw deep.

This concept ties heavy into Concept #20, which states that you must be sure to attack the upfield vertical distance of the football field with your passing game. In essence, you must be able to throw the football deep. You may not be able to throw the football deep as efficiently as when you throw short to intermediate passes. However, when you are able to complete deep passes, and your opponent knows you can, you will help prevent the secondary from attempting to "sit down" on shorter routes. You will have "blown the top" off of the coverage.

Where most offenses make mistakes in attempting to throw deep passes is that the football doesn't have to be thrown 50 or 60 yards downfield to be a successful deep pass. First of all, very few quarterbacks at any level can effectively throw deep passes that long. They may be able to pass the football that far. However, can they throw the pass with the proper height and drop in action that a deep pass needs to be successful? And, throwing an on-time, 42-yard (our goal) streak completion is as close to the definition of a streak pass completion as you can get. Even an open field fade completion (or a cover 2 hole throw completion) has the effect of giving up deep completion yardage by the defense—specially if the receiver is able to tack on yardage after his catch. Throwing a post or a post-corner route completion also helps to throw deep successfully. On all of these deep (or deeper) route passes, the quarterback *must* throw on time. A late throw often means that the receiver will outrun the effectiveness of a well-thrown deep pass—not necessarily the distance of the pass, but the pass's effectiveness.

A key to throwing deep is *to do it*. If you throw deep in games, then you will take the time to properly teach, coach, and practice the needed deep throwing and route running execution skills necessary to produce an effective deep throwing passing game. Deep throwing may never produce high percentage throwing. However, the "home run" effect helps greatly to produce points, build offensive moral, and help deflate the moral of the defense. And even when you have a deep pass incompletion, the defense now knows that it better stay deep.

Concept #48: Utilize double-move routes to throw deep and to complement base routes.

Another means of throwing deep is to use double-move routes. Hitch-and-go routes, slant-and-go routes, quick out-and-up, normal-out- or square-out-and-up, and curl-and-go routes can be extremely effective in helping a pass offense to throw deep. Some offenses effectively run go route action off of curls.

Double-move go and up route actions are a complement to the base (i.e., hitch) routes thrown. Go and up route actions work when secondaries "jump" the base hitch, slant, out, or curl route. Such double-move routes must be run deliberately. Proper shoulder turn (and, at times, receiver eyes looking back in towards the quarterback) makes a tremendous difference in helping to sell the base route and help set up the go, or up, action to gain deep passing yardage.

An excellent thought is to install (teach) any complementary double-move go, or up, route you intend utilizing on the day you install the complementary base route. In this fashion, you will then be installing the hitch (and go) concept, helping to develop a solid understanding of the interrelatedness of the base and double-move complementary route. That does not mean that the hitch and the hitch-and-go routes will receive similar practice repetition. After all, the base hitch route will be run in game situations far more than the complementary, double-move hitch-and-go route. However, throwing one hitch-and-go route for every seven or eight hitch routes helps the get the hitch-and-go route practiced off of an interrelatedness with its base route. Diagram 48-1 shows a variety of go and up double-move routes plus the Y-nod double-move route off of a Y-stick stem fake.

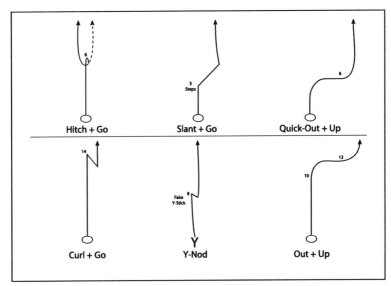

Diagram 48-1. Double-move routes

Concept #49: Versus zone coverages, receivers must find zone voids and throttle (stop).

Versus zone coverages, the receivers should look to find the zone voids and throttle down into the voids to receive the pass. The receivers throttle down (at times, stop) in the zone void so that they don't overrun, or run out of, the zone void. Actually, the receiver should throttle down as soon as possible when he enters a zone void. Doing so will allow the receiver to make the catch and turn upfield for addition yardage by avoiding the next zone defender who will be attempting to tackle him.

By "throttling down," it is meant that the receiver actually gears his speed down so that he can come under control to hang in the open void for the quarterback for as long as possible. Actually, the receiver should be studying the zone receiver nearest to the area where he is working his route. He does this to see if he can throttle down immediately as he passes that defender or if he has to continue into the middle of the zone void before he can throttle. The difference is the read of the shoulders and the drop of the zone defender off of which the receiver is working. If the dropping defender has his shoulders turned heavily to the outside and is breaking hard, the receiver can throttle down early as he passes the zone defender and enters the zone void. If that same defender has throttled down himself and has square shoulders to the line of scrimmage, the receiver must go to the center of the zone void to insure making the catch. The problem with working to the center of the zone void is that the receiver will be closer to the next zone defender in that defender's efforts to make a tackle.

Some coaches tell their receivers to actually stop in zone voids. Some routes—such as options, hooks, and curls—can actually force a receiver to stop in zone voids. Diagram 49-1 shows an in breaking receiver zone throttling off of a dropping zone defender.

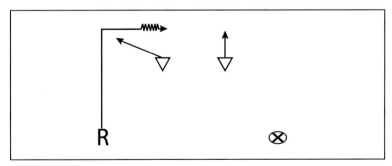

Diagram 49-1. Zone throttling an in breaking route off of a zone dropping defender

Concept #50: When the receivers separate from man coverages, they must maintain such separation.

The receivers must remember that once they use their man-to-man separation techniques to separate from a man coverage defender, they must then run at top speed to be sure to maintain such separation. They cannot make the mistake of man coverage separating and then zone coverage throttling into an open area once they have achieved such separation. They must remember the reason that they man-to-man separated in the first place. Throttling down after separation only allows the man coverage defender to catch up to the receiver rather than having the receiver maintain the separation distance by running at top speed away from the defender. Diagram 50-1 shows the concept of man separating from man-to-man coverage and the maintaining of such separation using an out-breaking square-out route for the example.

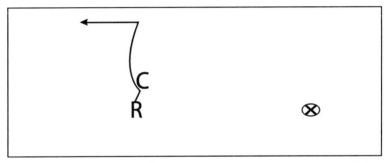

Diagram 50-1. Separating from man-to-man coverage and maintaining such separation (out breaking square-out route shown)

Concept #51: "Just get completions" versus man-to-man coverage.

When faced with man-to-man coverage defenses, the focus of the pass attack should be to "just get completions." To get desired pass yardage versus man-to-man coverages, short or deep, think to throw quickly to short and intermediate, on-the-move routes. Examples of such routes would be slants, quick posts, drags, drives, crosses, square-ins, square-outs and speed-outs (which will probably adjust to square-outs versus man-to-man coverages), and streaks. Due to the fact you are playing a man-to-man (or a predominantly man-to-man) coverage team, a quickly thrown (and caught) route to a receiver who is on-the-move can often lead to very successful yardage gains. As a result, simply getting completions, no matter how short of a throw distance that may be, can often be an extremely effective means of producing large chunks of passing yardage versus man-to-man coverages.

Much of this potential to produce large yardage gains versus man-to-man coverages is due to the ability of the receiver to run for yardage after the catch. Versus man-to-man coverages, you should make a big deal of man separating and maintaining such separation (Concept #50) so that you can get yourselves open to receive a pass. Another reason you should demand such man-to-man separation from the man covering defender is the tremendous potential for a pass receiver to run for additional yardage after the catch as a result of such separation. You could certainly think to throw to deeper, longer developing digs, post-corners, comeback-outs, and hook-type routes. However, quickly thrown passes require less pass protection time making pass protection and, as a result, the pass action easier to execute. Diagram 51-1 shows a quick slant isolation route in an effort to get completions.

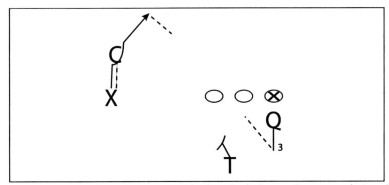

Diagram 51-1. Throwing to a quick slant isolation to "get completions" vs. man-to-man coverages

Concept #52: You must be able to beat bump/press man-to-man coverage.

Along with not being able to handle blitz, nothing can be more devastating to the effectiveness of a pass offense in general than not being able to handle bump/press man-to-man coverages. If a pass offense is not well versed in its attempt to defeat bump/press man-to-man coverages, it will have a difficult time succeeding. An offensive pass design must have a well thought out plan of attack in regard to pass patterns and routes to be utilized to defeat bump/press man-to-man coverages.

The receivers must be ready to execute their man-to-man separation techniques versus such bump/press coverage. They must utilize proper man stemming/stepping techniques, low pad-level control, and any needed hand release techniques to combat defensive jamming. The receivers must work the hips of the bump/press coverage defender in an effort to blow by, or away from, the defender. The quarterback must be ready to throw passes that tightly lead the receivers away from the bump/press man-to-man coverage technique. The receivers must then aggressively go and get the football. Timid, non-physical receivers will probably not fare well when faced with bump/press man-to-man coverages.

Concept #53: You must have aggressive wide receiver play.

Unfortunately, due to their physical stature, many wide receivers often are the physical weak links of an offense. However, physical stature can have nothing to do with physical toughness. depending on the attitude of a wide receiver. A wide receiver must be physical and aggressive on his releases, during his stems, on his separation techniques (especially versus man-to-man coverages) and in his ball catching skills. And. once the wide receiver catches the football, he must now become a tough, physical ballcarrier, refusing to be taken to the ground.

When the football is in the air as a result of a pass by the quarterback, the wide receivers must be able to play aggressively. They must aggressively go after the football. When the football is in the air, it is *their* football, not the defensive back's. If a fight for the football ensues, the receiver is the one who must "body up" on the football and physically overwhelm his opponent. The opposite cannot happen. Wide receivers cannot be the physical weak links of the offense. Instead, the wide receivers should strive to be the difference makers in regard to helping developing a tough, hard-nosed, physical offense.

Concept #54: Don't let the routes of a pattern bleed.

Route bleeding is the concept of some of the routes of a pass pattern getting too close to—or bleeding into—one another. As a result, the area around those routes becomes congested. Two routes may be so close to one another that one defender may be able to cover both receivers; or, put more simply, a bleeding of pass routes may bring too many pass defenders into the route bleeding area. Throwing a pass into congestion is a leading reason for interceptions. Pass pattern designs must space pass routes properly so that route bleeding is unlikely. Then, the receivers must have a thorough understanding of concept of proper route spacing and proper route spacing execution to ensure no bleeding of the routes. Diagram 54-1 shows an example of a pass pattern that produces route bleeding.

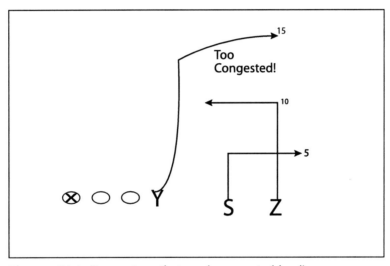

Diagram 54-1. Pass pattern that produces route bleeding

Concept #55: The quarterback must anticipate where he is going with his prime route read throws.

A quarterback can often find that he does not have time for elaborate, or delayed, route and pattern reading. As a result, the quarterback must be sure that he is anticipating where he is going to throw the football before it is even snapped to him by the center. Dropping back, planting the back foot, and then trying to make the proper reads will almost always lead to being too late.

From film study and from the teaching and practice of the game plan, the quarterback must have an idea of where he's going to throw the football when he breaks the huddle. If a speed-out route is the prime route called, the quarterback must be thinking how this route is part of the game plan to attack, say, the soft man free coverage or three-deep zone coverage that the opposition has shown in its scouting tendency breakdown. As he approaches the line of scrimmage, the quarterback checks to see if, indeed, it is the coverage he is expecting. While under center, he continues to analyze the defense. If his reads remain constant, the quarterback should now feel comfortable to take his quick, five-step timed throw dropback action to throw the speed-out. As he drops back, he uses his anticipation to make key reads to see if his pre-snap reads are correct. Barring any last second defensive reaction change, he can then plant his back foot and throw a well-timed, accurate pass.

Once again, waiting to make such a pass read determination *after* the quarterback sets up may be far too late in relation to strong pass rush efforts by the defense. Diagram 55-1 shows a quarterback anticipating throwing a curl route versus a cover 3 strong safety who works to the flat quickly.

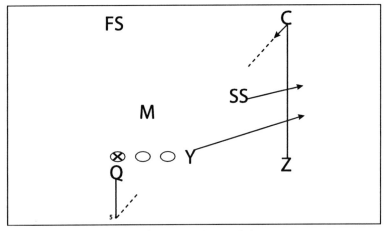

Diagram 55-1. Quarterback anticipating curl throw vs. cover 3 strong safety who works to the flat quickly

Concept #56: Use quick developing prime route read patterns.

To develop an efficient pass attack, it behooves the offense to throw to quick developing prime route reads. Quick developing three- and five-step timed patterns and route combinations need less protection time. Long developing route pattern combinations need longer pass protection time. Long pass protection time needs are a difficult chore when being pressured by heavy defensive rush threats. Therefore, a pass pattern that focuses on a prime route speed-out throw has a good chance of being efficiently thrown off of a quarterback's five-step timed plant-throw action. A seven-step timed prime route throw to an 18-yard dig route necessitates much more difficult pass protection needs due to the increased protection time that is required. The key is to throw to well designed, quick developing prime read routes and route combinations that allow for quick reads, quick throws, and quick prime route completions. Diagram 56-1 shows a quick developing speed-out prime route read combination.

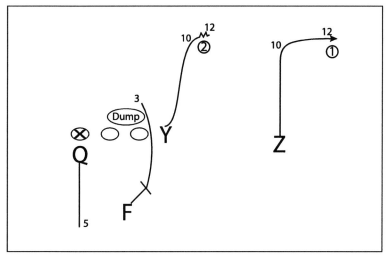

Diagram 56-1. Quick developing prime route read speed-out pattern

Concept #57: Use the important prime route concept.

The prime route concept is a very important concept to be mastered if a pass offense is to be effective. The prime route concept states that if a prime route is not open when the quarterback hits his plant foot, the quarterback should then get off the prime route read. Instead, he should go to his outlets.

The rationale for the prime route concept is that if the prime route read does not look good when the quarterback hits his plant foot, rarely does the prime route read get better. Actually, it almost always gets worse. This is especially true versus zone coverage since the defenders will probably have their eyes focused in on the quarterback's eyes. As a result, their positioning will have a tendency to shift to where the quarterback is looking. If the quarterback's initial read looks poor, it will probably only get worse as a result of the eye focus of the pass defenders. Conversely, as the prime route read becomes worse, the outlet reads almost always become better since the defense has shifted its focus to where the quarterback is initially reading with his eyes.

At times, the prime route read may just need a drop more time to come open. For this reason, the quarterback may want to stay with his prime route read for a short time more before scanning to his outlet routes. Diagram 57-1 shows the operation of the prime route concept with a curl/flat route combination.

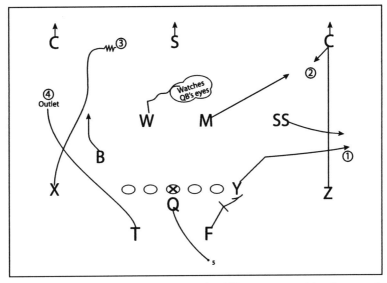

Diagram 57-1. Prime route concept (curl/flat route combination used for example)

Concept #58: Option routes are extremely effective one-on-one prime read isolation routes versus man-to-man or zone coverages.

Option routes, in which a tight end, back, or slotback receiver has the ability to man or zone break to the inside or outside, are extremely effective prime isolation routes. Quite simply, the option receiver has a four-way go working opposite the zone drop or the man-to-man coverage defender (usually a linebacker or nickelback) on whom they are isolated. Actually, some coaches give their option route receiver a five-way go option. On the fifth option, they can take their option route deep if no secondary defender is deep behind the receiver's stem point.

Versus zone coverage, the option receiver stops and sits in the zone void, inside or outside, opposite the nearness of the defender off of whom he is working. The option receiver actually attempts to stick his butt into (turn his back to) the face of the defender. He actually tries to screen the defender off from the pass with his body.

Versus man-to-man coverage, the option receiver man separates and stays on the move to maintain such separation away from the technique of the man coverage defender to the inside or outside. If the pass pattern design can produce a true one-on-one isolation, the option route has an excellent chance of getting open to provide an excellent prime route target for the quarterback to throw to. Diagram 58-1 shows a tight end one-on-one, Y-option isolation.

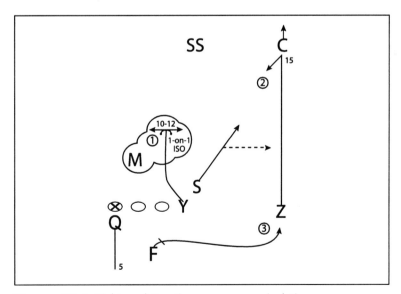

Diagram 58-1. Tight end Y-option one-on-one isolation

Concept #59: Work to create favorable one-on-one personnel isolation mismatches.

A very effective passing game thought is to work to create one-on-one route isolations that favor the offense from a personnel mismatch standpoint. The option route concept discussed in Concept #55 is an excellent means of creating one-on-one isolations in the favor of the offense. Formationing to have a quick tight end run his option route off of a slow middle linebacker or running a halfback option with a speedy tailback off of a slower linebacker are excellent one-on-one isolation mismatch examples.

Pitting a big, strong, talented split end versus a short, non-physical cornerback who may not be very talented with a rollaway route or speed-out route also greatly helps to create a one-on-one isolation mismatch in the favor of the offense. Isolating a tall receiver against a short cornerback with a fade route is another excellent example. Or, simply finding formations that force a defense to pit a defender with poor ability against one of the offense's best players is another. Diagram 59-1 shows a one-on-one isolation of a split end executing a streak route versus a press man free coverage cornerback while the flanker runs a deep rollaway outlet route isolation in an effort to create personnel mismatches in the favor of the offense.

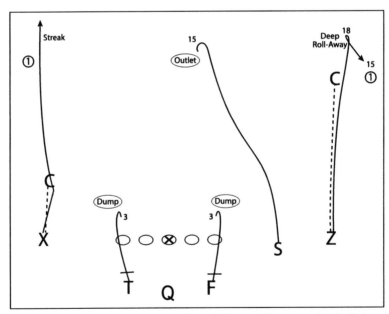

Diagram 59-1. One-on-one streak and deep rollaway outlet isolations to create personnel mismatches

Concept #60: Underneath delay, cross, scissor, and sit routes offer extremely effective control passing.

In the efforts of a pass offense to throw the football downfield, coaches often overlook the value of throwing to short, underneath control routes and route combinations. When defenses drop deep to get underneath deep and intermediate pass routes and patterns, they often leave themselves vulnerable to short underneath passing. Such routes and patterns have, in themselves, the ability to gain reasonable amounts of short yardage gains. It is often in the yards after catch ability of the delay, cross, scissor, and sit routes and their receivers that often make these routes and patterns extremely effective. Diagrams 60-1 through 60-4 shows examples of delay, cross, scissors, and sit routes and route combinations.

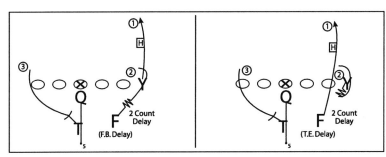

Diagram 60-1. Underneath delay routes for effective control passing

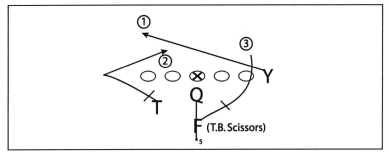

Diagram 60-2. Underneath scissor route combination for effective control passing

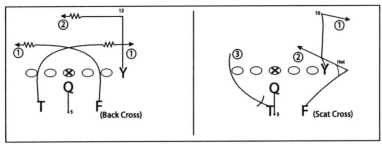

Diagram 60-3. Underneath cross route combinations for effective control passing

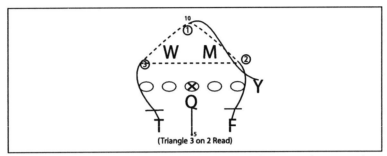

Diagram 60-4. Underneath three-on-two triangle sit read pattern for effective control passing

Concept #61: Outlets must be easy for quarterback to go to.

Just as in the importance of quick developing and easy to read prime route patterns, the outlets for the quarterback should also be easy to read and throw. The quarterback is often under too much pressure to have enough time to make difficult outlet reads.

The quarterback must understand that dumping off or checking down to short, underneath safety valve type outlets helps to avoid sacks. The quarterback must also understand that the reason such short outlet routes are often open is because the underneath coverage has dropped deeply underneath any intermediate and deep level routes being executed. As a result, a dump-off or check-down route throw may lead to a sizeable gain. A quarterback's quick read progression of "1 - 2 - dump" helps to turn potential sacks into safe and consistent pass completion gains. Diagram 61-1 shows an easy-to-go-to fullback/tailback dump outlet routes off of a blast play-action fake.

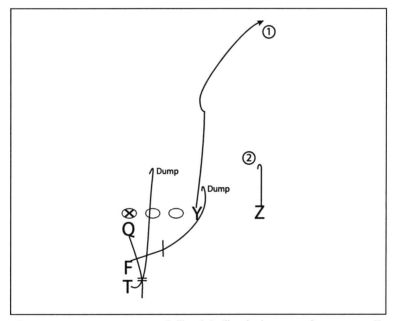

Diagram 61-1. Easy-to-go-to fullback/tailback dump outlet routes off blast play-action fake

Beside check-down, dump, safety valve type outlet routes, easy-to-go-to backside outlet routes can greatly help to produce effective outlet yardage gains. The key for such backside outlet routes is to have such outlet routes working to the inside into the quarterback's vision. In this fashion, when the quarterback scans to the backside, he will either see an open outlet receiver working to him or see a defender in front of such a receiver. Seeing a defender in front of the receiver would tell the quarterback that the initial backside outlet receiver is covered and that he should continue scanning outside to the next backside outlet receiver. Diagram 61-2 shows easy-to-go-to backside outlets that work inside into the quarterback's vision.

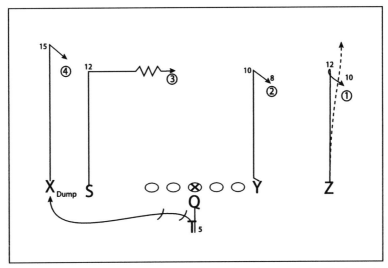

Diagram 61-2. Easy-to-go-to backside outlets that work inside into the quarterback's vision

Concept #62: The three-step quick passing game is one of football's most effective passing game series.

The three-step drop quick passing game is one of football's most effective passing game series. Many coaches would argue that it *is* football's best passing game series. The three-step drop quick passing game series is easy to protect, easy to execute, and has a consistently high pass completion percentage for those teams that use it as an important part of their total passing game design.

The three-step drop timed quick passing game does not rely on strong-armed throwing action by the quarterback. A major reason for this is that the quick game passes are normally short passes in length. Passing accuracy is normally more important in the quick passing game than arm strength. The short throw emphasis of the quick passing game helps allow for great control passing. Diagram 62-1 shows a quick-out pass pattern with inside-out quick zone pass protection.

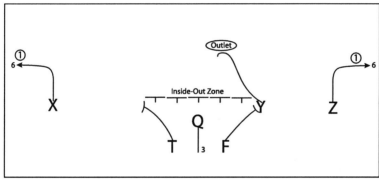

Diagram 62-1. Quick-out pass pattern with quick inside-out zone pass protection

Concept #63: Quick passing game protection is one of football's easiest and most effective protections.

The three-step drop timed quick passing game throws the football quickly—certainly one of its major assets. One of the reasons it is so successful is that the quick game pass pro blockers simply don't have to protect for long. Defenses find it very hard to get to the quarterback before the quarterback releases his pass. This situation is true whether the blocking scheme is man-to-man or zone. One way or the other, inside-out man or zone blocked quick pass protection (gap protection certainly can be utilized) seals off inside penetration. The blocking schemes leave any unblocked rushers to the outside. From such outside, widened rush alignments, it is difficult for pass rushers to get to the quarterback before he releases his pass—even if the rushers are left unblocked.

It is important for the offensive line to take on their blocks firmly, directly on the line of scrimmage. Cut blocking is widely used by many quick pass teams. However, the quick passing game blockers must be sure that their cut block actions are through the defenders' groin areas in an effort to buckle the defenders over the thrust of their cut blocks. Cutting any lower on a defender may enable a defender to jump over a cut block and/or keep his hands up to knock a quick pass down.

Concept #64: Move the quarterback launch point.

The use of the shotgun set (or formation) is a way to initially move the quarterback's launch point and help a quarterback versus pass rush pressure. This can be especially true for a short quarterback. The shotgun set in and of itself does not necessarily provide the quarterback with additional time to throw the football. However, on average, the shotgun formation should provide the quarterback with one more second of time to read the coverage and/or stunt/blitz pressures. In addition, the quarterback is in a better position in the shotgun to see, and therefore evade, rush and blitz/stunt problems.

Shotgun formations with two backfield blockers can help afford the quarterback the best possible protection. The blocking backs are in an excellent position to block their assigned defender. In addition, they are in an excellent position to help clean up on any rusher who comes free if the back's assigned defender does not rush.

Moving the quarterback's launch point from under the center or from the shotgun set (move-out, roll-out, sprint-out, dash, bootleg, etc.) helps to move the quarterback away from the backside of a pass rush. In addition, such move action slows the pass rush down since the pass rushers have the additional pass rush concern of having to find out where the quarterback is actually going to set up or move. This action must be done while still attempting to beat the pass blocker assigned to him. Diagram 64-1 shows a moving of the quarterback launch point action to help versus pass rush pressure.

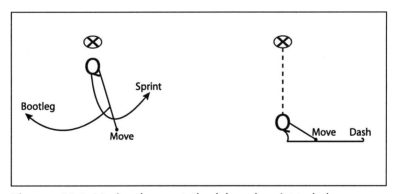

Diagram 64-1. Moving the quarterback launch point to help vs. pass rush pressure

Concept #65: Use sprint out run/pass option attack.

The use of pass plays utilizing run-pass option sprint-out action by the quarterback can be an extremely effective offensive concept. Much like run option football, an entirely new dimension is placed upon the defense, the option run action potential of the quarterback. Sprint-out pass action is the most direct form of the run-pass option pass plays. It is the most direct because the quarterback attacks the line of scrimmage right off the bat to put a definite run threat on the defense. This thought is magnified greatly if the quarterback is a good running ballcarrier.

Whether it is sprint-out, roll-out, dash, bootleg, or naked bootleg action, a quarterback breaking outside onto the perimeter as he attacks the line of scrimmage puts tremendous stress on the coverage defenders. Does the defense come up to stop the quarterback's run threat and open up an easy throw to a receiver? Or, do the defenders stay in coverage and allow the quarterback to run for a sizeable yardage gain? Much like run option football, the defense is forced to become much more assignment oriented. Diagram 65-1 shows sprint-out run-pass option action with double rollaway routes by the wide receivers.

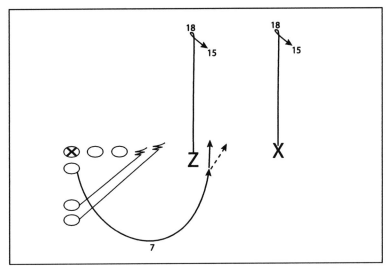

Diagram 65-1. Quarterback run-pass sprint-out action with double deep rollaway routes

Concept #66: Use a variety of pass protections.

It is important to use a limited variety of pass protections within your offensive pass design. Using one basic pass protection, however, may not be enough to properly block a defense. If a defense knows that the offense only uses one basic pass protection scheme, it will be easy for the defense to dissect and attack an overly simplistic pass protection design. Having two base dropback protections (or a base dropback pass protection scheme and an alternate dropback pass protection scheme), a quick passing game protection scheme and two (perhaps three) play-action pass protection schemes can help create a diverse, well rounded pass protection package. Such a tight knit pass protection package can allow an offense to protect its quarterback while having great diversity in its overall pass attack. If an offense's pass protection package is to add an additional or alternate protection, it should be some form of an easy stunt/blitz beater protection. An example of such an easy stunt/blitz beater protection is the full zone gap protection shown in Diagram 66-1.

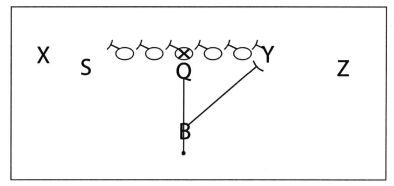

Diagram 66-1. Easy full zone gap pass protection to block stunt/blitz

Unfortunately, the problem that many offenses have is not that they have too little in the form of pass protections. Instead, it is that they have too many pass protections. Pass protecting is not easy, nor is it simple—especially when one considers how offenses often have to block a multitude of fronts, stunts, and blitzes. Once again, simplicity is the key. When in doubt, cut back. Having too many pass protections can quickly lead to confusion. A confused offensive line will have a greatly reduced chance of pass protection success.

Concept #67: An offense must be able to beat stunts and blitzes.

Offenses must be prepared to handle stunts and blitzes. If an offense is not prepared to handle stunts and blitzes, a defense can absolutely over run an offense. Nothing is more devastating to an offense than not to be able to handle a stunting/blitzing defense whether the stunts/blitzes have man-to-man coverages behind them or are zone blitzes—especially if the offense does not have answers and is not well prepared to combat such pressure.

An offense can attack a defense's stunt/blitz game in a variety of ways. No matter what type of anti-blitz design an offense may have, an offense must have a plan of attack to account for the stunt/blitz games and coverages they may see. Hot routes and sight adjustment routes can be effectively utilized depending on the yardage the offense realistically needs to get. When faced with stunting/blitzing defenses, offenses should utilize their best pass protections. Maximum protections, in which the offense blocks with seven (even eight) blockers can be considered depending on the type of stunts/blitzes and stunt/blitz coverages seen.

The quick passing game can help exploit short- to medium-depth underneath zones. They can quickly help put the football underneath the arms of receivers who may be able to gain sizeable yardage on a vertical route. Much of that yardage can be gained as a result of the receivers running with the football after the catch. Man coverage beater pass routes and patterns—such as crossing routes, fades, and out routes—can be utilized to effectively beat stunting/blitzing man coverages. Screens can be checked to effectively combat heavy stunt/blitz pressure—especially those coupled with man-to-man coverages. An offense can overload block the end of line of the defensive front and utilize sprint-out type pass action. Such sprint-out action helps the offense to run away from backside stunt/blitz pressure.

Whatever the anti-blitz design an offense may have, it must have answers. It must have a sound plan to handle pressure every time it steps on the field versus an opponent. The offense must be well versed and well practiced in its anti-blitz package so that it has the ability to attack and dismantle any attempt to stunt or blitz it.

Concept #68: The quick passing game is, in itself, an excellent blitz beater package.

The three-step drop timed quick passing game is an excellent blitz beater package because of its quick route and pattern structure, which effectively attacks both man-to-man and zone coverages. It is also the result of its firm, inside-out, on-the-line-of-scrimmage pass protection design (gap protection can also be effectively used). In addition, with the football being thrown so quickly, the blockers do not have to block for long. When rushers do come free, it is normally from the outside, where the greater distance to the quarterback prevents the rushers from getting to the quarterback before he is able to release his pass. Doing so helps to keep any free rushers from rushing through the inside in the face of the quarterback.

The quick passing game does not have to be adjusted, or checked out of, when faced by stunting or blitzing defenses—other than to, perhaps, signal or check to a particular route or route combination due to the coverage seen. Quick-outs, hitches, slants, and fades are excellent blitz beater routes. In addition, the quarterback could hold an additional blocker in (such as the tight end) to provide extra protection versus an all out blitz by the defense. Other than that, the quick passing game is, in itself, a highly effective means of handling stunts and blitzes.

Concept #69: Attack blitz pressure with fast developing prime read route(s).

Slow developing routes and patterns put tremendous pressure on the pass protectors due to the need to hold up for a long period of time. When faced with blitz threats, the offense has added protection difficulties. A sound means of combating such blitz pressure is to utilize pass patterns built around prime read routes that develop and come open quickly. Such routes, in themselves, can be used as blitz beater routes.

Fast developing prime read routes help give the quarterback a better chance of delivering his pass. The pass patterns utilized should provide easy prime reads for the quarterback so that he can get the pass off quickly. The pass patterns shouldn't fear utilizing prime routes that may require the catching receiver to have to run for additional yardage to get the needed yards. Diagram 69-1 shows a fast developing rollaway prime route read combination for the quarterback with a back's short alley route in an effort to attack blitz pressure.

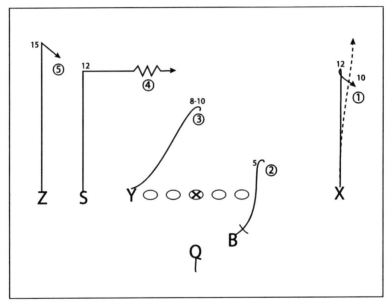

Diagram 69-1. Attacking blitz pressure with fast developing rollaway prime route read combination

Concept #70: Use blitz beater routes within your pass pattern design.

Another method that can be utilized to beat the blitz is to use routes within the workings of your integrated route patterns which can act as effective blitz beater routes. As a result, specific routes within a pattern's design are designated as blitz beater routes for the quarterback to go to once he sees blitz pressure. The receivers who run the designated blitz beater routes must be aware of such blitz beater needs as they release off the line of scrimmage. Diagram 70-1 shows the designation of the tight end's cross route as the pattern's blitz beater route.

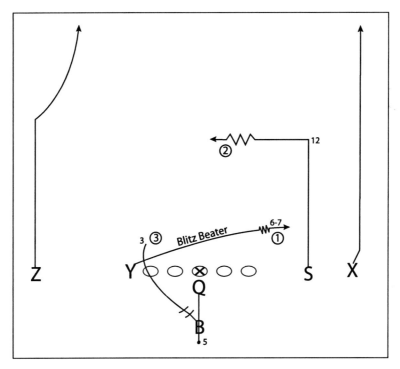

Diagram 70-1. Using the tight end's cross route as the blitz beater route within the pass pattern design

Concept #71: Built in blitz beater routes to the backside of the prime route(s) is an effective blitz beater concept.

To combat an excessive use of the blitz by your opposition, you can tack on blitz beater routes to the backside of the prime route combination reads. As a result, the quarterback stays with the prime route read side if he does not read blitz. If the quarterback does read blitz, he then focuses on his blitz beater route to the backside. Such a concept eliminates the needs for sight adjusting, maximum protections, or the need to audible and check to another play. Diagram 71-1 shows a curl-flat prime read concept to one side with a drag blitz beater route read to the other.

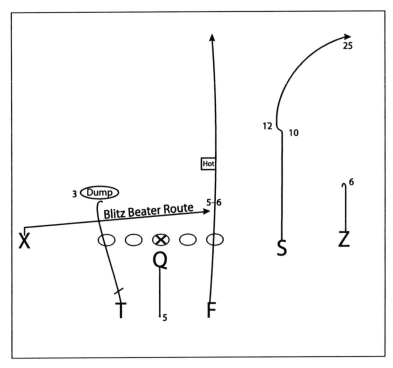

Diagram 71-1. Prime route read to one side and a blitz beater route read to the other

Concept #72: Hot route action can help to create excellent stunt/blitz control.

The use of hot route action can be a very effective means of helping to control stunt/blitz pressure by a defense. Inside attacking linebacker and nickel/strong safety stunts and blitzes can be controlled by free releasing backs, tight ends, and inside slotted receivers. Instead of being blocked by one those offensive players, the football is "dumped" (thrown) to such a receiver if the defender the free releasing receiver is assigned to stunts/blitzes. Diagram 72-1 shows such a hot action as the quarterback throws a dump pass to the tight end when the strongside inside linebacker, to whom the tight end is assigned, stunts to the inside. The hot action dumps the football to the tight end into the vacated area left by the stunting linebacker.

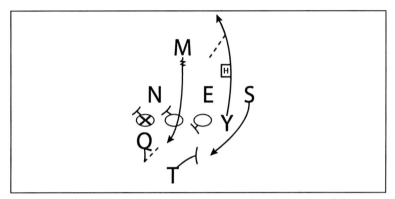

Diagram 72-1. Tight end hot route action to produce stunt/blitz control

Concept #73: Sight adjusting is an excellent blitz control system.

The use of sight adjusting is an excellent means of controlling secondary blitzes. A sight adjustment is an on-the-move adjustment of a normal intermediate or deep route. The route is adjusted to a quickly timed one- to three-step timed route action by the quarterback and wide receiver to the side of the blitzing defender. Once the quarterback and receiver see ("sight") the blitz action, an automatic, on-the-move adjustment is made by both offensive players.

Different offenses have different sight adjustment rules. Many start out by building their sight adjustment systems off of the philosophy: "Slant until you can't." If the sight receiver can't slant, then other adjustments are made such as fades or an almost-on-the-line-of-scrimmage hitch route. Diagram 73-1 shows short hitch sight adjustment action versus a cornerback blitz by the quarterback and split end. The split end does not run a slant route due to the low positioning of the free safety in an effort to take away a slant sight adjustment route.

Diagram 73-2 shows sight adjustment action to a slotted formation versus a strong safety blitz. From such slotted formation, both receivers are shown executing sight adjustment slant routes.

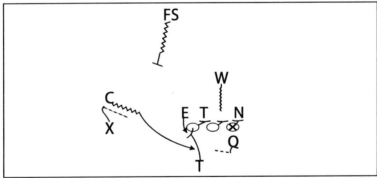

Diagram 73-1. Sight adjustment action (short hitch) vs. cornerback blitz with low free safety

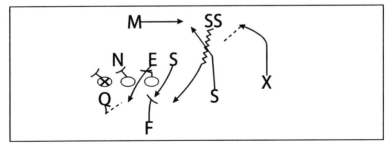

Diagram 73-2. Sight adjustment action (double slant) vs. strong safety blitz to slotted formation

Concept #74: Have maximum seven- and eight-man protections to block blitzes.

The use of seven- or eight-man maximum protections utilizing only two or three prime receiver route patterns is an excellent concept to utilize versus defenses that blitz. Maximum protections help to best combat overloaded blitzes. Seven- and eight-man blocker protection can be used to ensure that the quarterback can have the time needed to effectively throw his pass. A variety of such seven- and eight-man blocker protections can be utilized for all types of pass action—from play-action to dropback.

Even though the main focus of such protections is to protect the quarterback and give him time to throw, possible check-release action by the backs and tight ends should still be kept in mind. Free blockers can be kept in to help other blockers. However, blockers releasing into pass routes when their blocking assignments drop into coverage can greatly help to affect the coverage scheme, be it man-to-man or zone. Diagram 74-1 shows a seven-man maximum zone gap protection with the back and tight end having check-release route potentials. Diagram 74-2 shows an eight-man maximum man protection in which the fullback becomes the "clean-up" blocker picking up any extra blitzer to either side of the football.

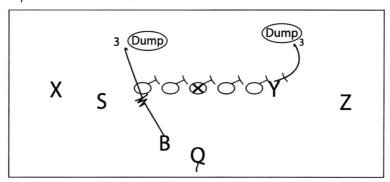

Diagram 74-1. Seven-man maximum zone gap protection with check-release capabilities

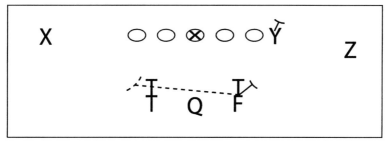

Diagram 74-2. Eight-man maximum man protection with extra clean-up "blocker"

Concept #75: Seven-blocker shotgun man protection with "clean-up" blocker may be the best maximum pass protection for the dropback passing game.

The seven-blocker maximum man protection from the shotgun formation with a "clean-up" blocker to pick up the extra blitzer may consistently be the best of the maximum protections. A major reason for this is that few defenses all-out blitz with eight defenders. From the shotgun formation, the two backfield blockers are in an excellent position to check their onside blocking assignments and still be in position step across the formation to block to the opposite side to pick up an extra secondary blitzer. In addition, from the shotgun formation they are in an excellent position to be late "help" type blockers to assist block on any late developing rushers that other blockers may be losing. As a result, the wide receivers have no need to sight adjust.

The protection scheme is a man protection designed scheme with big-on-big blocking assignments. The two backs check their linebacker to an outside blitzer on their side to a backside blitzer. After checking those assignments, the backs can stay in to help other blockers or be put on check-release route assignments. From the shotgun formation and an up stance, the backs can be taught to easily see safety rotation as the snap count cadence begins to be called by the quarterback. This sequence can help tip off blitz action and to which side the blitz is coming. (The secondary normally rolls its coverage to the side of the blitz.) Diagram 75-1 shows the maximum seven-man shotgun protection with "clean-up" blocker for a weak corner crash blitz from a reduced Eagle defense.

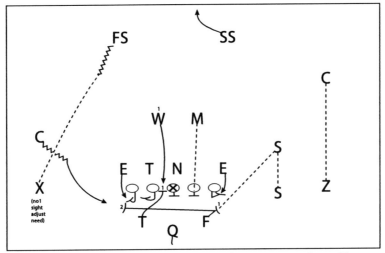

Diagram 75-1. Maximum seven-blocker shotgun protection with clean-up blocker vs. outside blitz

Concept #76: Screens effectively help to slow down pass rushes and can be excellent blitz beaters.

Screens, just as draws, are perfect complements to the passing game. They feed off of the efforts of the defense to rush, pressure and sack the quarterback. The greater the upfield pressure, the better the situation for a screen's development. Screens are an extremely effective means of combating the heavy use of stunt and blitz pressure. Well-executed screens can effectively burn such stunt and blitz pressure for big gains. Many teams will actually check to screens as a part of their blitz/pressure beater repertoire—especially versus man coverage blitzes.

Screens can come in a multitude of designs, actions, and timings. When most people think of screens, they think of screens developing off of dropback pass action. However, screens can develop off of move actions by the quarterback, as well as off of play-action pass fakes. Timings for screens can range from quick developing screens off of one- to three-step drop action by the quarterback to slow developing screens off of naked bootleg action. And, screens can come off of a double screen design in which a quick screen is run to one side of the formation and a slower developing screen to the opposite side.

Screens demand a commitment. Much like effectively throwing deep to streak routes, executing effective screens takes a lot of work. Much of screen development can be practiced in a team (or unit) period "on air." Two offensive units can rapid fire practice a multitude of screen repetitions, one unit after the other, with the linemen who release downfield blocking on large bell blocking dummies. Practicing "on air" allows the entire offensive unit to develop the sense of timing that is so important to the execution of screen designs. Keeping it simple demands that quantity of offense always being kept in mind when developing a total offensive package. However, the greater the emphasis of the passing game in an offense's overall design philosophy, the more a coach may want to think about screen diversity as a part of that philosophy.

Diagram 76-1 shows double screen action from a balanced one-back doubles formation. Initially, the quarterback reads the rush of the end-of-line defender to the back's flare screen. If the end-of-line rusher rushes the quarterback, the quarterback throws the flare screen over the top of the rusher as he hits his fifth drop step. If the end-of-line rusher peels out wide to cover the flare screen back, the quarterback pump fakes the flare screen action, retreats two more steps, and throws a speed screen to the split end to the opposite side. Diagram 76-2 shows a slow developing naked bootleg play-action pass screen.

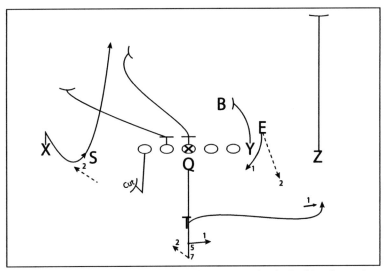

Diagram 76-1. Double screen action from a one-back doubles formation

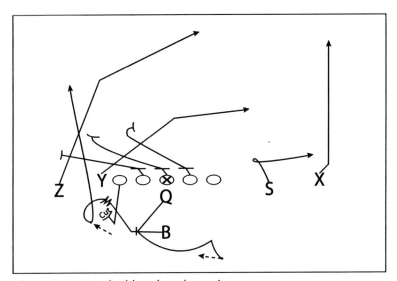

Diagram 76-2. Naked bootleg play-action screen

Concept #77: Shovel passes effectively help to slow down heavy pass rush efforts.

Shovel passes are an extremely effective way to slow down heavy, penetrating pass rush efforts by the defense—especially when the shovel pass is executed from the shotgun formation. The problem for the defense, once the ball is snapped to the quarterback in a shotgun formation with the backs stepping up to show pass block action, is that the defense gets a true pass read. With the linebackers now being influenced to take pass drops, the defensive front becomes more vulnerable to the shovel pass block design. A key for the execution of the shovel pass is to be able to seal any heavy pass rush penetration that should be expected. Penetration can readily interfere with and disturb any pulling linemen utilized in a shovel pass blocking scheme. Diagram 77-1 shows a shotgun formation shovel pass versus a 4-2 nickel defense. A key block is the block of the backside pulling guard. If the end-of-line defender sits on the line of scrimmage, the pulling guard kicks the defender to the outside. If the end-of-line defender penetrates hard upfield playing the quarterback, the pulling guard disregards him and pulls up inside to become an extra blocker for the linebackers, or possibly a safety.

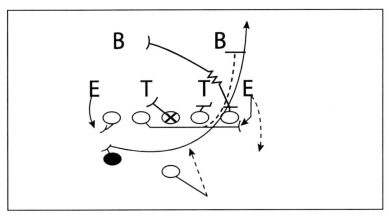

Diagram 77-1. Shotgun formation shovel pass vs. 4-2 nickel defense

Concept #78: Play-action passing is the complete complement of the running and passing games, tying the two together.

Play-action passing is the complementary action that ties together an offense's running and passing game. Play-action passing has the running and passing games feeding off one another to be successful. A good run fake holds and influences linebackers—and in some cases the secondary—to distort pass coverages and create advantages for the passing game. Many coaches consider play-action passing the best type of passing as a result. The only real limitation to the effectiveness of play-action passing is the strength of the actual run threat as a result of the down and distance and/or the game situation. A play-action pass fake on third-and-13 may have little effect on linebackers and secondary defenders. A hard faking play-action pass on third-and-three in the middle of the fourth quarter of a close game will probably have an extreme effect on the play of the defense helping to create an easy pass completion.

The best play-action pass plays, for the most part, come off of a team's best run plays. A defense must gear itself to stopping an offense's best run plays if it is to successfully stop the opposition's run game. As a result, play-action passes that develop off of an offense's best runs have the best chance of influencing the defense.

Hard inside run fakes help to hold linebackers to help make the defense vulnerable to intermediate and deep pass patterns. The linebackers are held up from dropping effectively underneath such throws. Quick inside and outside "flash" type fakes can hold linebackers and secondary defenders for the split seconds that will allow receivers to outflank the coverage or get them open vertically on quick upfield "pop" routes and slants. Bootleg play-action passes can help provide offenses with effective crossing route play-action passing and help add vital misdirection to boot. When a coach examines his own offense, the potentials for play-action passing are almost unlimited. When an offense blends its running and passing game together, it can create a dynamic play-action package that can greatly enhance the effectiveness of an offense's overall design. Diagram 78-1 shows a play-action pass action off of the sprint draw with a split end dig route as the prime read route.

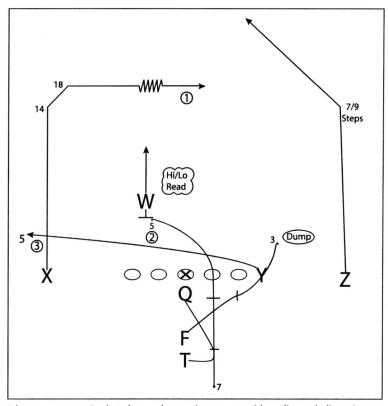

Diagram 78-1. Sprint draw play-action pass with split end dig prime read route

Concept #79: Misdirection (naked) bootleg passing is tough to stop.

Year in and year out, one of the most effective pass play-action pass series in football is the misdirection (naked) bootleg series. Actually, it may consistently be the most effective pass series in football period—play-action or not.

The (naked) bootleg pass is extremely effective due to the fake of full flow run offense to one side and misdirection bootleg action to the other. The full flow run fake action—be it sweep, inside zone, outside zone stretch, or any other type of full flow run fake—has a tremendous influence on producing hard run pursuit flow by the defense. Such hard run pursuit allows the receivers to work across the formation to the backside bootleg action where not much coverage is often remaining. The quarterback bootlegs away from the run action fake to the outside to be a run/pass option threat. Misdirection is very hard on a hard run pursuing defense and the (naked) bootleg play-action passing can help produce as good a misdirection action as you can get.

The difference between bootleg and naked bootleg action is whether or not the offensive design pulls a playside (run fake side) offensive lineman (probably a guard) to the backside—the side of the quarterback's bootleg action. On a pure bootleg play-action pass, a playside lineman is pulled to seal block the end of line defender. Doing so enables the quarterback to break contain and run with the football to the outside if his receivers are covered. If the end of line defender rushes upfield to contain the quarterback, the pulling lineman is able to protect the quarterback for an inside set-up point approximately over the tackle area by kicking the upfield rush defender to the outside. Diagram 79-1 shows bootleg action versus a reduced Eagle defensive front.

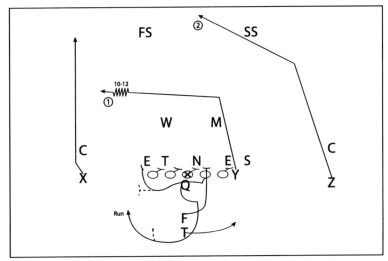

Diagram 79-1. Bootleg action vs. reduced Eagle defensive front

On naked bootleg action, no lineman is pulled to the backside to lead—and protect—the quarterback. On pure naked bootleg action, the end-of-line defender is left unblocked. Such naked bootleg action should be run when the end-of-line defender pursues the run fake hard and flat down the line of scrimmage. Diagram 79-2 shows pure naked bootleg action.

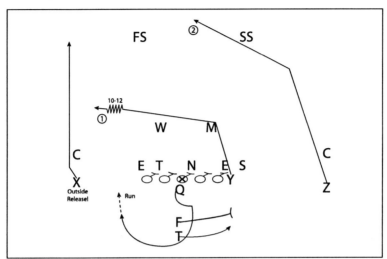

Diagram 79-2. Naked bootleg action vs. reduced Eagle defensive front

Another popular way to run naked bootleg action is to have a back slam the unblocked end-of-line defender before releasing into a flat route as part of the naked bootleg pass pattern. Or, a tight end can work to the flat off of fake reach block action. Slam-flat action by a back on a naked bootleg is shown in Diagram 79-3.

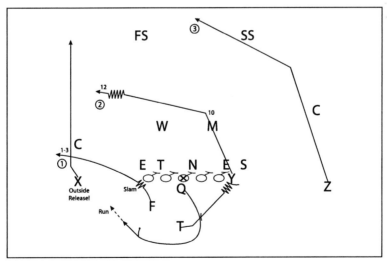

Diagram 79-3. Naked bootleg action with back slam-flat route vs. reduced Eagle defensive front

Concept #80: A pass offense must have a built in scramble concept.

During the course of a football game, chances are good that your quarterback is going to drop back to pass and be forced to scramble from his launch point due to a heavy pass rush and/or poor pass protection. What does your pass offense do now? Watch the quarterback scramble? That's not a good answer. What the receivers should do is to adjust their routes from the called pass pattern and execute a designed scramble pattern.

The scramble concept is just that, a designed pattern of adjusted routes that work towards the scramble action of the quarterback in a designated fashion. What is the designated scramble fashion? That's up to the coaching staff and the scramble pass pattern concept and rules that the staff designs.

Diagram 80-1 shows a scramble pattern design off of rules which state that if a receiver is to the side of the scramble and is deep, he should work back to the quarterback. If a receiver to the side of the scramble is shallow (or in an intermediate zone), he should take his route deep. All other backside receivers should trail across the formation in an effort to find a window for the quarterback to be able to throw them the football.

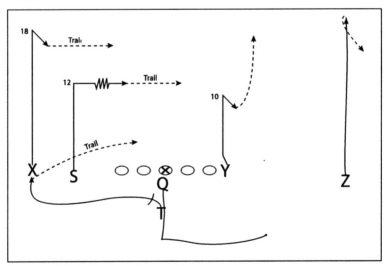

Diagram 80-1. Designed scramble concept

A trailing receiver must never "climb up the back" of another trailing receiver. If a trailing receiver finds that such a "climbing the back" action is happening, he should redirect upfield for five yards and then break back into a new trailing course ("stair step") in his efforts to create a window for the quarterback to be able to throw him a pass. Diagram 80-2 shows such scramble "stair step" action to avoid climbing the back of another trailing receiver.

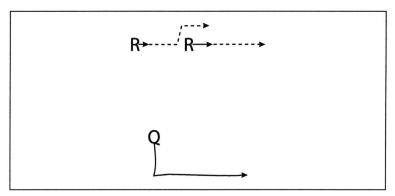

Diagram 80-2. Scramble concept stair step action on a trail route

One last scramble concept thought to consider is: if the quarterback is forced to scramble back to the opposite side of his initial scramble, the scramble rules (whatever they may be) should, simply, be reenacted to the opposite side.

An offense's scramble concept should be taught and practiced. An excellent way to practice the scramble concept is to tell the quarterback to set up, make his normal pattern reads, and then scramble to one side or the other to force the pass receivers to enact their scramble concept rules. Do this on one seven-on-seven, skeleton pass drill repetition and on one team period pass play repetition. Just two repetitions a day can help to properly practice and develop an all-important passing game technique—especially if the practice is being videotaped to provide an excellent teaching tool of the concept.

Concept #81: Using your two-minute, on-the-line offense as a change of pace can be an excellent concept.

Using your two-minute, on-the-line offense as a change of pace in a normal, non-critical offensive situation can be an excellent concept—especially if the offense seems to be stale in its execution (out of rhythm) and needs something to shake it up a bit. On-the-line offense in a non-two-minute offensive situation, helps present the defense with a new sense of offensive timing to have to defense in a situation where they are not expecting to see such action.

In using the offense's two-minute, on-the-line offense in a normal, non-critical offensive situation, the offense does not have to do anything differently than they would if they were in a normal, two-minute, on-the-line offensive situation. The offense is able to utilize a change of pace offense that is already a big part of their offensive design and already well practiced and developed.

Concept #82: Attack a defense's weaknesses.

Any defense that an offense will face will have strengths and weaknesses. It is important to find a defense's weaknesses through your scouting analysis efforts. Then, utilize your game plan to find the run and pass plays in your arsenal that can exploit such weaknesses. In essence, you want to go for the defense's jugular and outright attack the defense's weaknesses.

The defensive weakness may be a particular defensive player, or the inability of the defense to defend against a certain formation and/or personnel plan. The defense may show a definite weakness to inside runs, or sweeps, or option plays. The defense may show that it is extremely vulnerable to play-action passes and misdirection bootleg-type plays. Whatever the weaknesses you see in the defense, you must be sure that you attack those weaknesses. You must develop a plan to attack such weaknesses. Once you have developed and practiced such a plan, you must be sure that you are disciplined in your play calling efforts to enable your offense to execute that plan and truly go for the defense's jugular.

Concept #83: Attack a defense's strengths.

As has been previously mentioned, any defense that an offense will face will have strengths and weaknesses. The defense's strength may be a particular player, or two or three players. The strength might be the use of a particular defensive front or a particular type of blitz package. Whatever the strengths of the defense, an excellent way of handling those defensive strengths is to find ways to actually attack those strengths.

Versus a great defensive tackle, an answer might be to run away from that great defensive lineman. However, if he really is a great player, he will probably find a way to pursue across the formation and still be a factor. Attacking that player by double-team blocking him over and over and over again during the course of the game, running the football right behind that double-team action, can negate the effectiveness of that great player. Or, if the great defensive lineman is a great upfield pass rusher, trapping him a good number of times might effectively slow down his upfield rushing efforts. Disrupting the play of a great player cannot only greatly disturb the effectiveness of that specific player, but the entire defense as well. Take out the "spark plug" of the defense and the defense may be sorely affected—both physically and mentally. If the defense's strength is a certain part of its defensive front, find plays that effectively hurt the defensive front's strength and use it repeatedly. Finding a way to hurt a defense's strength is a great moral booster for an offense and a great moral disrupter of a defense.

Concept #84: Get the football in the hands of your best players.

If you want to consistently have an effective offense, rely on the abilities of your most talented players. Who are your best receivers? Find effective ways to throw them the football. If facing blitz pressure and man-to-man coverage is a strong possibility, which of your receivers are best at beating pressuring man-to-man coverages? Which receivers are best at beating bump/press coverages? Is your tight end a great receiver? Then find ways to get him the football. Is your fullback a slow, tough blocking back and your tailback a great ballcarrier? Then give the ball to your tailback and let your fullback lead the way. Don't put those two different types of backs in a split back formation and expect them to equally carry out mirrored run and blocking roles. Run a reverse with your speediest, best reverse runner. He may not be your best receiver. However, if he's your best reverse runner, let him run your reverses.

Whether run or pass, find ways to put the ball in the hands of your players who have the most magic to get the ball in the end zone. Maximize your chances to score by getting the ball in the hands of the players who have the best abilities to get the job done. Make sure you use whatever magic you have to its fullest capabilities.

Concept #85: Use your best/most effective plays.

As important as it is to put the football in the hands of your most talented players, it is equally important to use your best plays. Statistically, your best plays are usually the ones you use the most. They are the ones your players have the most experience using. They are the plays your players know the best. Your most used plays are the ones your offense has probably practiced the most in the need to get them game ready.

Conversely, at the end of the season, analyze all of the plays you used five times or less. What you will normally find is that those rarely used plays are your most inefficient, ineffective plays during the course of the season. Why? For one reason, they were probably an afterthought. They were probably plays that were included in your playbook "just in case." Or, they were plays you added because they looked good on video in someone else's offense. Utilizing new and/or seldomly used plays may very well end in futility because the offense may not know how to run those plays versus the wide variety of defense they may see.

Use the plays your players know (and execute) the best. If anything, even cut down on your base repertoire by eliminating all but the best of the base plays of the offense, run or pass. The key is to run your best, most effective plays. Those are the plays your players know the best and have the most confidence in. Those are the plays that will allow your offense to best attack whatever a defense may throw at it.

Concept #86: Be sure to vary your snap count.

One of the worst mistakes an offense can make is to utilize one, consistent snap count. Utilizing one snap count—as overly simplistic as that may seem—plays hugely into the hands of the defense. The snap count cadence should be a weapon for the offense. Not knowing when the football is going to be snapped from the center to the quarterback keeps the defense guessing. The defense is not able to jump the snap count because they don't know what it is. This forces the defense to react to the movement of the football and the offenders rather than having any snap count knowledge advantage.

The quarterback must be sure to be disciplined in the multiple usage of his snap-count system. An offense's snap-count system can be an effective weapon if it is allowed to. Conversely, it can be of great detriment to an offense if not used properly.

One of the reasons that offenses are not good at utilizing a multiple snap-count cadence system is that the coaches don't give it the proper chance to develop. Coaches are so concerned with having a great first practice in pre-season that the offense is told to initially only go on its most basic snap count. Since the singular snap-count cadence worked well for the first practice, it will probably be utilized for the second, the third, and the fourth. Before you know it, the first scrimmage is at hand and very little of the snap-count cadence system has been installed. Then comes the first pre-season game and, still, little of the total snap-count cadence system is game ready because it was never given the chance to properly develop.

The best way to install your snap-count cadence system is to install it all in the first practice (or at least in the first two or three practices). Such thinking will probably produce rough snap-count execution for the first practice and probably for the first few practices. However, after a week or so of rough line-of-scrimmage snap-count cadence usage, the system suddenly starts to come together well as the players get used to it. By the first game, the snap-count cadence system is well practiced and well developed. It now becomes ready to be a season-long weapon for the offense as the offense is able to control the line of scrimmage with its multiple snap-count system.

Concept #87: Use trick plays.

Much as hating to see run option offense, defenses hate to face an offense that runs trick plays. Trick plays are scary for defenses. Defenses are often forced to expend inordinate amounts of time preparing to defense trick plays because of their, often, big play capabilities.

Trick plays do add volume to an offense. However, if they are kept in a small series (or package) of special plays that are practiced in an occasional, but consistent, practice pattern, they can be a very effective in adding to the total effectiveness of the offense. As with the practice of screens, practicing trick plays can be an excellent first period drill of 10 minutes or so that helps to get the offensive players' blood flowing. Or, the trick plays can be used as a conditioning drill at the end of practice with the execution of the trick plays followed by all players running a set amount of yards after the completion of a trick play execution. By developing such a package of trick plays in the pre-season, a trick play or two can be easily activated for a specific game against a specific opponent.

Trick plays are fun for both the players and coaches and should be viewed that way. If they are, the players will be motivated to execute the trick plays properly to help add their big play potentials to their overall offensive design. It's fun to practice, coach, and execute a reverse pass play off of one of your option plays or a throwback to the quarterback off of sweep action. Diagram 87-1 shows a throwback to the quarterback double pass trick play.

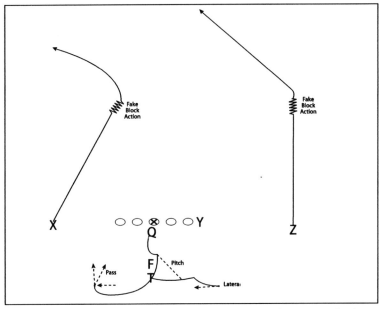

Diagram 87-1. Throwback to the quarterback double pass trick play

Concept #88: Be unpredictable in your play calling.

An excellent means of helping to produce an effective offense is to be unpredictable in your play calling. Your opponent is hoping that just the opposite will be true, which is why defensive staffs spend so much time on opponent evaluation of an offense's play calling tendencies. Good defensive staffs analyze the play calling tendencies of an offense in every area of the field—when the football is on a hash mark or in the middle of the field, on down-and-distance situations, and in critical situations such as coming-out offense or two-minute offense. The defensive staff hopes to find definite tendencies by the offense so that they can overload and attack such tendencies. Running the football on every first and second down and then passing only on third-and-long is a defensive signal caller's dream. Unfortunately, it's amazing how many offensive play callers do call a game that way.

Be unpredictable. Run a trap play on third-and-long and throw a play-action play on third-and-short. Now make sure the quarterback has an easy check-down receiver sitting in front of him to throw to for the first down if the deeper prime route is not open on that third-and-short situation. However, if the defense jumps on the third-and-short play-action run fake, you may find that your offense has just scored a long touchdown rather than just gaining the short yardage needed for the first down. Defense is very rhythmic and is very hopeful that the offensive play calling will be predictable. Running (or throwing) the football on every first down plays right into the hands of the defense. Use your play call ready list to create a varied mixture of runs, play-action passes, and dropback passes. That doesn't mean that if your opponent can't stop your best play, your off-tackle power, that you should run other plays to just be versatile or unpredictable. However, coupling your off-tackle power with your misdirection runs and play-action passes that come off the off-tackle power will help to make your offense—and the off-tackle power—all the more potent.

Be a wheeling, dealing riverboat gambler when it comes to play calling. Don't let the defense know what has hit them. Keep your opponent in the dark by not giving them tendencies which they can hang their hat on in their efforts to stop your offense. Be unpredictable.

Concept #89: Teach and coach fundamentals.

As has already been stated, *what* you do is important. However, *how* you do what you do is much more important. Another way of putting that is that your players must be able to execute what you are asking them to do. Yes, they must know their assignments well. However, knowing the assignments but not having the technical skill to execute those assignments will most likely mean failure.

Your players must be able to execute their techniques. To do so, they must be able to have a sound base of fundamentals to allow them to execute. Positional fundamentals are the basis of any offense. Without strong fundamentals, execution chances are extremely limited. No matter how sophisticated, multiple, or diverse your offense is, it will have little chance of succeeding unless your players have a strong fundamental base on which to rely.

Teach and coach the needed fundamentals of your offense—and teach and coach them well. A common complaint of many coaches in today's game is that defenses—and, as a result, offenses—have become so sophisticated and complex that little time is available for fundamental development once the game season actually starts. If that's true, then maybe it's time to cut back on the volume of what you are doing. Maybe it's time to not be so sophisticated, multiple, and diverse. What's the sense of having the latest, high-tech offense if your players don't have the technical skills—the fundamentals—to execute it? To have a championship-caliber football team, you have to be able to block and tackle. That fact hasn't changed since the inception of the game. To have an effective, efficient offense, you need to block, throw, catch, secure the football, and carry the ball. Those are fundamental skills that your players need to master no matter what type of offense you have. So, yes, what you do on offense is important. However, how you do what you do will ultimately determine whether or not your offense will—or will not—be successful.

Concept #90: Refuse to tolerate mistakes.

As an offensive coach, you must refuse to tolerate mistakes. Such a statement may not sound like much of a revelation. Of course, you, as a coach, should not tolerate mistakes. However, how often in a team period will you see an obvious mistake and, other than a quick verbal rebuke, see the offense go directly on to the next repetition. Perhaps the error is a player jumping offside, a missed assignment, or an incorrect application of a blocking scheme.

How do you not tolerate such mistakes? First of all, you could simply repeat every play repetition that does not meet the coach's satisfaction. You might be on the practice field until midnight if you did that, you say. That certainly could be possible. It would also be very unrealistic. However, when a player jumps offside, immediately replacing that player with his substitute and immediately having him do 25 "up downs" helps to reinforce the fact that you, as a coach, are not going to tolerate mistakes. In addition, the rest of the offense seeing the player who jumped offside being "rewarded" with the 25 up downs helps to reinforce the fact that you are not going to tolerate mistakes to the entire offense.

There are a number of ways to help ensure that you are not going to tolerate mistakes. The last 10- or 15-minute period of a practice may be reserved for corrections. If a team period repetition is executed incorrectly or poorly, the coach yells out, "Put it on the correction period list!" If the offensive players practice poorly, the entire extra 10- or 15-minute correction period will be utilized. If few (or no) mistakes are to be practiced again, the offensive players are rewarded with a shortened practice. As a result, practicing for quality—rather than just quantity—is not given mere lip service.

You can find many imaginative ways to not tolerate mistakes. Perhaps the aforementioned correction period can be made into the end of practice conditioning period. Each repeated practice repetition may have 40 yards of sprint action tacked on to the end of a correct repeat of the plays needing fixing. If few (or no) play practice repetitions need repeating, the offense could be rewarded for efficient and effective practice by not having to perform whatever conditioning regimen that they otherwise were scheduled to do on that day. As a result, your offense may miss some, or most, of its conditioning work that day. However, the tradeoff is a great practice.

Concept #91: Teach the rules.

Teach your offense the rules of the game. Penalties are one of the greatest deterrents to effective offensive football. A means of helping to be a penalty-free (or reasonably penalty-free) offense is to emphasize the importance of understanding the rules of the game. If you are a multiple formation team, it is extremely important to understand that a wide receiver cannot cover up a tight end on a pass play. It is extremely important to understand that you cannot block a defender in the back and how you can avoid doing so. What are the rules for crackback blocking? What constitutes offensive pass interference? What is an illegal chop block? What is illegal substitution?

Your offensive players need to understand the answers to these questions. They must understand the rules and they must be made to understand the importance of knowing the rules. A good way to emphasize the rules to your offensive players is to pull out the rulebook and test them occasionally. Two or three rules questions may be an excellent way to open an offensive unit meeting. Or, asking such questions at the unit meeting the night before a game may be an excellent opportunity to emphasize the rules. Cutting out a conditioning wind sprint for a correct answer to a rule's question is a fun way to teach the rules under pressure. However you do it, teaching the rules can pay big dividends towards the effectiveness of your offense.

Concept #92: Emphasize ball security.

A number of times at clinics, I have heard coaches say that you cannot coach a ballcarrier to not fumble. This is about as incorrect of a concept as you could find in football coaching. You can *definitely* teach and coach a ballcarrier not to fumble and must definitely do so if you expect to have an effective offense.

The technique for properly carrying a football is that the football should be locked under the ballcarrier's armpit. The index and middle finger should straddle the tip of the football and squeeze it into the ballcarrier's armpit. (The ballcarrier should *not* carry the football with his index finger over the tip of the football. Such action can help promote fumbling if the ballcarrier receives a blow to the index finger as he is being tackled.) The elbow should be wrapped underneath the football to help squeeze the football into the ballcarrier's armpit. No "air" should be showing between the football and the ballcarrier's armpit. Such an "air-tight" ball security technique may actually slow a ballcarrier's running speed down a drop. That's all right. The fastest ballcarrier in the world can't be very effective unless he can secure the football while running.

An excellent way to emphasize, teach, and coach proper ball security is to have one individual period assigned to ball security drills every day—or at least have one quick ball security drill every day. Specific drills to practice the center/quarterback exchange, the exchange of the football between the quarterback and a ballcarrier, and the securing of the football after a catch must be utilized. In unit and team drills, ballcarriers cannot be allowed to run with the football and show "air" between the football and the armpit. If they do, they need to be "rewarded" with "up downs" or "push ups" to help remind them of the importance of proper ballcarrying techniques. And if the ballcarrier were to fumble, the "reward" should be even greater. Much as was stated in Concept #90, mistakes cannot be tolerated. Similarly, poor ball security cannot be tolerated.

Concept #93: Practice sideline personnel substitutions and play calling communications.

An often overlooked (but extremely important) practice and developmental concern is sideline personnel substitutions and play calling communications. How often do you watch a game on television and see a quarterback calling for a time out because the wrong personnel has come in from the sideline or because he didn't get the play call that was sent in correctly. Or, perhaps, the formation and/or play signal from the sideline wasn't seen clearly by the quarterback, resulting in a delay of game penalty. Whatever the problem, sideline personnel substitutions and play calling communications must be "air tight" and efficiently executed during the course of a game. In addition, they must be done in a timely manner so that the quarterback and offense have plenty of time to affect any needed blocking calls and/or check to specific play calls. Unfortunately, far too many coaches spend far too little time on such sideline personnel substitution and play calling mechanics in practice.

The key to effective sideline personnel substitutions and play calling communications is to practice those mechanics in as game-like of a practice situation as possible. Take 10 to 20 minutes of practice time to send your offensive personnel to the sideline with only your 11 starters on the field. Be sure to practice on a well-lined field to help create a full, game-like situation. Down-and-distance markers and situational play calling can be used to make the drills even more specific. Now execute the unit or team period off of your practice script sending in all personnel substitutions and play calls (signaled or run in) from the sideline. The coaches who normally send in the needed personnel, and send in (or signal) the plays, should be the coaches on the sideline for the drill.

The player/messenger bringing in the play call must lip-read *all* of the coach's call to heighten focus and concentration. The messenger cannot turn his head away from the coach sending in the play until the coach is completely finished giving him the play call. The player/messenger now sprints to the huddle, locks on to eye contact with the quarterback, and carefully enunciates *all* of the call. The messenger must be sure to not turn his head away from the quarterback until *all* of *his* call is complete. The quarterback lip-reads *all* of the call from the messenger and then *carefully* enunciates *all* of the call to the players in the huddle. Such precise play call communication practice is what eliminates costly mistakes come game time.

The effect of the drill can be heightened by actually using your scoreboard to utilize a game and play clock. A coach or manager should operate the clock. The drill can go so far as to have the play calling coaches actually go up to the coaches' press box booth to practice communications through the phone system as they would during an actual game.

During the drill, a wide variety of the personnel plans should be used as well as the formations, shifts, motions, and plays to be utilized. Any difficult substitutions and/or formation/play calls should be especially practiced. If certain plays are put on a wristband for the quarterback, those plays should be practiced as well to insure that the quarterback is comfortable with the wrist band system come game time.

Many coaches dislike coaching this way because they are on the sideline, or up in the booth, and not able to see what their players are doing close up during the drill practice. It must be remembered that the focus of the drill is sideline personnel substitutions and play calling communications. The extra bonus of coaching fundamentals and execution must come from viewing and teaching off of practice video.

Concept #94: After a tight base run and pass package, all additional plays should be critical situation need plays.

Concepts #26 and #43 spoke about the importance of having nice, tight run and pass packages. They told us to have a limited number of base runs and pass patterns. They then told us to complement those base runs and pass patterns with other runs and passes to help produce a balanced offense for defenses to have to contend with. The use of misdirection run and pass plays was an excellent example of supplemental run and pass plays to the base plays to help create a complete, base offensive design that fully attacks the field horizontally and vertically. It was then said to stop. Instead of adding other run plays and pass patterns, wait until you evaluate your critical situation needs before you add another thing. Why? Because any additions to your base offense should now come from those specific critical offensive situation needs.

What is meant by additional runs and pass patterns for specific critical offensive situation needs? Any specific runs or pass patterns that you may need for third down offense is an example. Are there any new, specific runs or pass patterns you feel you must have for third-and-short? Third- and-medium? Third-and-long? How about in the red zone versus all of that red zone blitz pressure? Are there any runs and pass patterns you must have to combat such heavy blitz pressure and man-to-man coverage? How about when your back is to the wall on your own two-yard line? Is there anything else you specifically need for your coming-out offense? Your slow down offense? How about the goal line? Your two-minute, on-the-line offense? Your desperation offense? Your kill-the-clock offense?

These important critical offensive situation needs are the additional runs and passes that you should add to your base offensive package and design at this point. Is it an off-tackle power play for third-and-short? Is it a special maximum pass protection for red zone blitzing? How about a specific deep pass pattern for third-and-long? Whatever you truly need for such critical offensive situations is what you should now add to your base offensive design to create your total offensive package. (For a complete guide to concepts for effective critical situation offense, see *Coaching Critical Situation Offense* by Steve Axman.)

Concept #95: Create critical situational packages for your offense.

Quite often, when an offense succeeds in a game and helps its team to victory, it was because it was successful in the game's critical situations. Par downs (first-and-ten, second-and-short to -medium) are relatively easy situations for a play caller to make his calls. Now third down? That's definitely a different story. The pressure is on. Succeed on third-and-medium and your offensive series continues. You are able to continue on your march towards your opponent's end zone. Fail and your team is punting the football away. Calling plays on third down, in the red zone, on the goal line, in a two-minute situation, or when your offense's back is to the wall trying to execute its coming-out offense are the toughest situations there are for a play caller. The same is true when you're in a slow down, or slow-slow, critical offensive situation or when you have to use your desperation offense to take a last shot at desperately scoring to pull out a victory. Even kill-the-clock play calling can be critical when every second your kill-the-clock offense can burn off the clock may be the difference in whether you can end the game with a victory or have to punt the football back to your opponent, giving them one more chance to pull the game out for themselves.

In the off-season, you need to develop packages of play calls which include possible formations, shifts, and motions for each of the critical situations that has been mentioned. These packages should come from your base offense whenever possible. Additional plays should be added only when necessary. As a result, you will develop a general critical situation play call package, or ready list, for all third-down situations (third-and-short, third-and-medium, third-and-long, and third-and-long-long). These should include a coming out package as well as a game-plan-ready list package for two-minute offense, the red zone , the goal line, and all the other critical offensive situations. Such critical situation packages should be practiced and developed in the pre-season. When the season actually arrives, the critical situation packages are adjusted for each opponent to the actual defensive structures the offense expects to see. The plays are culled from the general package ready lists to create specific critical game plan packages for each critical situation for each game. If additional plays are needed versus specific opponents, then such plays are added to the actual packages. (For a complete guide to concepts for effective critical situation offense, see *Coaching Critical Situation Offense* by Steve Axman.)

Concept #96: Practice situationally in as game-like of a situation as possible.

Practice your critical situation offensive packages in as game-like of a practice situation as possible. Practice your coming-out offense by placing the football on your own two-yard line during the team periods you have set aside for coming-out offense versus your opponent. Practice your coming-out offensive package versus the coming-out defense you expect to see from your scouting report information. On the day you practice third down offense, cover your third down package in your pre-practice meetings and in any pre-practice walk-through periods you may have. Practice your third down routes and route throwing in your individual periods. During your seven-on-seven pass skeleton drill, bring out the down marker and chains to set up as realistic a critical third down situation as possible. Practice your third-and-short, -medium, -long, and -long-long passes from your third down critical situation pass package ready list. Have a scout squad enact the defensive coverages you expect to see from your opponent on those critical situation third downs. During your team periods, set aside some of the periods for similar third down situational practice.

Thursday (if your games are on Saturdays) may be perfect day to practice your two-minute offensive package—including your two-minute, on-the-line offense. Again, practice such a critical situation offensive package in as game-like of a situation as possible. For the two-minute offense critical situation, be sure to use a full, well-lined football field. Make sure managers have the down marker and the chains out on the field to help simulate the down-and-distance. Use the scoreboard's game and play clock, if possible. Practice your two-minute offense personnel substitutions and play calling communications—including press box phone communications.

Whatever the critical offensive situation being practiced, it must be practiced in as game-like of a situation as possible. The important concept, however, is that you do specifically practice each of your critical situation offensive packages. They must be game ready to help your team win when faced with each, all-important critical situation. (For a complete guide to concepts for effective critical situation offense, see *Coaching Critical Situation Offense* by Steve Axman.)

Concept #97: Have a last play sequence game ready.

You must have a "last play" sequence ready for the end of the game (or of the half) when no time outs are left and three (or less) seconds are remaining on the clock. With precious few seconds left on the clock and no timeouts left for the offense, the quarterback must take the situation into his own hands and execute a well planned and well practiced last play sequence ready list.

After a play in which a first down has been achieved and the clock is going to restarted once the referee has reset the chains, the quarterback must be ready to execute his last play ready list if three (or less) seconds are remaining on the clock. If four seconds or more are left on the clock, the quarterback should immediately call for a "clock-clock" (or "spike-spike") play. At three seconds, the quarterback strongly risks the possibility of the clock running out on a "clock-clock" play. If three or less seconds are left on the clock, the quarterback must go to his pre-designed last play sequence ready list.

The last play ready list reflects where the football is on the field. A good breakdown is to have a last play call ready from the plus 21-yard line out, from the 20- to the 11-yard line, from the ten- to the two-yard line, and inside the two-yard line. A coaching staff, however, may decide to develop their own last play sequence yard line parameters. The actual plays that make up this last play ready list are either established for the season, or weekly for each opponent. Since these are last play calls, the emphasis is play calls that will best give the offense a chance to score a touchdown.

An example of such a last play ready list might be a four-streaks pass pattern play from the 21-yard line or beyond. The emphasis here would be for the quarterback to pass to the streak receiver he feels has the best chance to make the catch and score. From the 20- to the 11-yard line, the last play ready list might be a double smash pass pattern play with the inside receivers to both sides running post-corner routes. From the ten- to the two-yard line, the last play ready list might call for a double inside receiver option route pass pattern with both outside receivers running fade routes. (The option route receivers would have to be sure to execute their option routes over the goal line.) Or, a draw-type run play could be utilized. When inside the two-yard line, the last play ready list might call for a quick passing game pattern, such as a double slant. Or, perhaps, a lead option run play might be part of the thinking in this situation. On all of these last play ready list plays, again the emphasis is on setting up a situation that will produce a touchdown with a reception, or a run play that will have an excellent chance to score.

It is important to reiterate that with three or less seconds remaining on the clock—and no time outs available—it is up to the quarterback to make the proper last play sequence call according to the position of the football on the field. There just might not be enough time on the clock for the quarterback to look to the sideline to try to get a last ditch play call signal amidst all the end of game excitement and get it properly communicated to the rest of the offense before the clock expires.

Concept #98: KISS (Keep It Simple Stupid)!

One of the most often used sayings in football coaching is KISS (Keep It Simple, Stupid). Almost every coach will agree that "KISS!" is a key concept to good coaching. If this is true, then why do so many coaches merely give lip service to this all-important concept? Most coaches do believe in the validity and importance of keeping it simple. However, a tremendous number of those coaches, in practice, do not keep it simple for their players.

What you do offensively is important. However, how you do what you do is far more important. The most sophisticated of offensive designs can be virtually useless if your offensive players cannot execute what you want them to do, due to lack of understanding. Sophisticated? That sounds like something a coach who wants to impress other coaches would want to claim, rather than a coach who is focused on getting his players to effectively execute an efficient, effective offensive design.

In a number of the concepts in this book, the idea of getting the defense to "frown" has been discussed. A confused, over-thinking defense has a tough time flying around, pursuing to the football and succeeding. Such a thought is no different for the offense. A confused, over-thinking offense can easily "short fuse" mentally, getting in the way of desired execution. When an offensive player knows, precisely, what he is supposed to do and how he is supposed to do it, he can feel confident to "let it rip" in an effort to dominantly execute his assignments.

Keep it simple, stupid. Present your coaching information in a concise, condensed, and uncomplicated format. Teach and coach to the players who comprise the most challenging segment (i.e., those for whom learning is the most difficult) of your offense. Why? Because some of those players may very well be your most talented players. If they don't have a firm understanding of what they are supposed to do, your chances of success will probably be greatly diminished. Your offensive playbook should look like a well-written, informative comic book with easy-to-understand diagrams rather than a telephone-book-sized encyclopedia volume. The encyclopedia volume may be jam-packed with tremendous coaching and teaching information. In reality, what such a large, highly technical text may be best for is a helpful resource for the coaching staff. Give your players a well-written, basic, clear presentation of your offense with precise, easy-to-follow diagrams and illustrations. Once your players have developed a sound, basic understanding of your offense and their roles and assignments, you can always add needed additional lessons of important information. Building on a strong, basic understanding is far easier than trying to help a confused player understand what he needs to be an effective player.

Teach concepts. Teach the "whys" and "hows" of every assignment—not just the assignment. Refine your system every year. Find subtle ways to make it better. You do not have to change your entire offense every year. How can you expect your players to master your offense if the offense is radically changed from year to year. Continuity helps to breed familiarity and confidence. Remember, it is not always *what* you do that is so important. Much more importantly, it is *how* you do what you do that, in the end, will make the ultimate difference. So, KISS (Keep It Simple, Stupid)!

Concept #99: Luck is when preparation meets opportunity.

Did you ever notice that the best teams seem to be the luckiest teams? Or more precisely, the best-prepared teams seem to be the luckiest teams? Luck is when preparation meets opportunity. How well is your offense prepared? Is it prepared for first down? For third- and-short? Third-and-long? Is your offense prepared for the red zone? For the goal line? Are your offensive players prepared to succeed when the football is on the one-yard line with their backs to their own goal line? How about two-minute offense? Desperation offense? Plenty of opportunities arise to succeed in a football game. The offenses that are the best prepared to meet such opportunities will almost always be the luckiest.

Concept #100: Great offenses make it happen.

Great offenses make it happen. They do not sit back and watch it happen to them. They know what they want to do. They are well prepared for all of the situations that may occur during the course of a game, and during the course of a season. They know how to make game adjustments when needed to ensure victory. The offensive philosophy is embedded in an offensive design that allows the offense to attack a defense's strengths, as well as its weaknesses. Great offenses have a built-in flexibility to find a way to combat and defeat efforts to shut down its best run and pass plays. Great offenses make it happen because they find ways to make it happen.

Concept #101: And...have fun when you coach offense.

Hey! Don't forget: football is a game. Supposedly, the reason you play games is to have fun. And what better way to have fun than to coach offensive football. What better way is there to have fun than to be able to sit in a staff room with your coaching friends and peers and design and formulate an effective offensive package? What can be more fun that to sit in a darkened staff room with those same coaches and break down and evaluate game video of your opponent to develop a winning game plan that can attack and dismantle an opposing defense? And, what can be more fun than to be able to go out on the practice field and coach your offensive players to become the best they can be?

Coaching offensive football is fun. Doing something that is fun is extremely motivating. It helps you to want to do and accomplish more. Having fun coaching offensive football is fun for you (as a coach), the rest of the coaches, and the players as well. When you're having fun, the necessary hard work doesn't seem to be quite so hard to do. Not enjoying coaching offensive football, the greatest game in the world, is a big mistake for you, your coaches, your players, and everyone else involved with your team. Remember, what could be more fun than coaching offensive football?

About the Author

Steve Axman was, most recently, the wide receivers coach at the University of Washington, a position he assumed prior to the 2004 season. It was Axman's second stint on the Huskies staff. Previously, he served as the assistant head coach, wide receivers coach, and quarterbacks coach at the University of Washington (1999-2002). As the Huskies quarterbacks coach, Axman oversaw the work of UW record-setting quarterbacks Marques Tuiasosopo and Cody Pickett. During the 2003 season, he was the offensive coordinator and quarterbacks coach at UCLA.

Axman is no stranger to wide-open, multiple offense football or producing top-flight collegiate quarterbacks. During his career, he has worked at four Pac-10 schools (UCLA, Arizona, Stanford, and Washington). Among his former collegiate pupils are Troy Aikman and Drew Olson (UCLA), Neil O'Donnell (Maryland), and Jeff Lewis and Travis Brown (Northern Arizona).

In 1998 (prior to joining the UW staff the first time), Axman served as the quarterbacks coach at Minnesota under Glen Mason. Before that, Axman was the head coach at Northern Arizona from 1990-97. He inherited a NAU program that had experienced just three winning seasons during the 1980s and had never qualified for the Division I-AA postseason playoffs. During his eight years with the Lumberjacks, Axman guided the team to a 48-41 record, making him the second-winningest coach in Northern Arizona's history.

Axman's NAU teams were known for their offensive fireworks. During his eight-year career, Axman's teams averaged 30 points per game. His 1996 Lumberjack squad set or tied 14 national records and averaged 43.2 points per game en route to a 9-3 overall record and a 6-1 record in the Big Sky Conference. That season produced a second-place finish in the Big Sky, the school's first postseason appearance, and a school-best No. 6 national ranking. In 1989, Axman served as quarterbacks coach for Maryland, where he worked with O'Donnell. In 1987-88, he was the offensive coordinator at UCLA, where he coached Aikman. Prior to UCLA, Axman coached at Stanford (1986), with the Denver Gold of the United States Football League (1985), and at the University of Arizona (1980-84), as the offensive coordinator and quarterbacks coach. Axman previously spent a year at Illinois, three seasons at Army, and one season at Albany State. Prior to that, Axman's first collegiate coaching assignment was at East Stroudsburg State in 1974. A 1969 graduate of C.W. Post in Greenvale, NY, Axman went on to earn his first master's degree from Long Island University in 1972 and his second in 1975 while coaching at East Stroudsburg State.

Axman has authored eight instructional books on football. He has also been featured on seven well-received instructional videos on football. He is nationally renowned for his knowledge of offensive fundamentals, schemes, and techniques, particularly quarterback play.

A native of Huntington Station, NY, Axman and his wife, Dr. Marie Axman, an elementary school principal, have four daughters: Mary Beth, Jaclyn, Melissa, and Kimberly.